THE CAMPAIGN
—— for ——
Woman Suffrage
IN VIRGINIA

THE CAMPAIGN
— for —
Woman Suffrage
IN VIRGINIA

BRENT TARTER, MARIANNE E. JULIENNE & BARBARA C. BATSON

THE
History
PRESS

Published by The History Press
Charleston, SC
www.historypress.com

The Votes for Women banner courtesy of Sophie Meredith Sides Cowan.

First published 2020

Manufactured in the United States

ISBN 9781467144193

Library of Congress Control Number: 2019951906

CONTENTS

FOREWORD

One hundred years ago, American women won the right to vote with the passage and subsequent ratification of the Nineteenth Amendment to the United States Constitution. The movement to secure woman suffrage began in the mid-nineteenth century, but it took many decades of hard work before a majority of Americans fully acknowledged that a country that denied half its population a voice in choosing their leaders and shaping the nation's future could never be regarded as a true democracy.

The story of the national effort to secure woman suffrage is a well-known and important one. The names of those who led the movement—Susan B. Anthony, Elizabeth Cady Stanton, Lucretia Mott and Carrie Chapman Catt, among others—are familiar to anyone who has taken a high school or college course in American history. The campaign for woman suffrage would not have succeeded, however, if its only focus had been at the national level, on Congress and the White House. The work that women did in statehouses across the country to persuade their local representatives to support the cause was crucial in turning the tide of opinion. Women banded together in their state capitals but also in their home communities, large and small, to make their case with their friends and neighbors. Over time, their work ensured the grass-roots support that state and national elected officials could no longer ignore.

The Campaign for Woman Suffrage in Virginia describes in vivid detail how the suffrage movement unfolded in a key southern state where traditional views about women (and much else) held sway. Despite the challenges they faced, Virginia suffragists created an effective state organization, the Equal Suffrage League of Virginia, that coordinated the efforts of scores of local chapters located not only in urban areas but surprisingly in remote and rural areas of the state as well. The suffragists in this book are for the most part unknown to historians of Virginia, and their achievements have not been properly understood. Indeed, they succeeded rather than failed in their original objective of persuading the General Assembly to propose a woman suffrage amendment to the state constitution

This book helps us understand who these women were and how they developed the practical arguments and strategies they believed would work with those they needed to convince. Here we also see the divergent opinions of white Virginia suffragists as they debated whether their goal should be an amendment to the state or to the federal constitution, whether their tactics should rely on persuasion or militancy and how to address the issue of race in a state that had substantially disfranchised its black male citizens. Because African American women had to work more quietly than their white counterparts to avoid a backlash that might jeopardize the cause, their contributions to the suffrage movement in Virginia have often been overlooked. *The Campaign for Woman Suffrage in Virginia* presents their efforts on behalf of social justice and suffrage as an important part of the story.

Virginia did not ratify the Nineteenth Amendment until 1952, a symbolic gesture, as Virginia women had been voting and participating in government affairs for more than three decades. By that time, many Virginia women profiled here had made their mark in the state's public life.

—Sandra Gioia Treadway
Librarian of Virginia

ACKNOWLEDGEMENTS

We thank former Library of Virginia archivist Jennifer Davis McDaid, who organized the Equal Suffrage League of Virginia Records and created the first finding aid; Library of Virginia archivist Trenton E. Hizer, who prepared the Equal Suffrage League Records for scanning and prepared a new finding aid for the collection; Kathleen Jordan, digital initiatives and web presence director of the Library of Virginia, who facilitated the digitizing of the records; Sophie Meredith Sides Cowan of Blue Hill, Maine, and Tucson, Arizona, who preserved and shared with the Library of Virginia the Virginia branch records of the Congressional Union/National Woman's Party; all the people who volunteered to research and write biographies of Virginia suffragists (and a few women who opposed woman suffrage) for the Library of Virginia's online *Dictionary of Virginia Biography*; and Sandra G. Treadway, Megan Taylor Shockley, Frances S. Pollard, Lauranett Lee, Gregg D. Kimball, Catherine Fitzgerald Wyatt, John G. Deal and Leila Christenbury, who read the first draft of the book and offered valuable suggestions.

LET OUR VOTE BE CAST

AN INTRODUCTION

"This is the proudest day of my life!" a woman in Norfolk, Virginia, exclaimed on November 2, 1920, as she prepared to vote for the first time. "The proudest day?" asked another woman who was waiting with her in line at the polling place. "Why, have you forgotten your wedding day?"

"No," the first woman replied, "but the Lord gave me the graces that won for me a wedding day, but it took more than God-given graces to bring about this day!"[1]

It had taken many years of hard work by deeply committed women in their hometown of Norfolk, elsewhere in Virginia and throughout the United States. About seventy-five or eighty thousand women, both black and white, eagerly went to the polls in Virginia that day to vote in what everybody agreed was a remarkable event, a turning point in Virginia history—a turning point in American history, too, because on that day for the first time, women in every state exercised the right to vote.

Women who campaigned for woman suffrage regarded the vote both as a natural right of citizenship and as a tool with which to achieve political objectives. Many of them worked for changes in local, state and national laws for the benefit of women and children to improve education, public health and conditions under which working men and women lived. Lillie Mary Barbour, a Roanoke member of the United Garment Workers of America and an advocate for working women, explained during the campaign that "the ballot in our hands is the only thing to help us."[2]

The woman suffrage movement was one of a sequence of campaigns that different groups of Americans fought to make a reality out of the implied promises of the Declaration of Independence and the Virginia Declaration of Rights that all men were created equal. When Thomas Jefferson and George Mason wrote those influential documents in 1776, they used the word *men* and referred to members of the political nation—adult, white men who owned property—but other Americans sought to be included. Much of the history of the United States and of Virginia can be understood as those other Americans' efforts to make a reality of the revolutionary promise. That promise drove the campaign for the abolition of slavery and for universal white manhood suffrage before the Civil War, to enfranchise African American men after the war, to win the vote for women late in the nineteenth and early in the twentieth centuries and powered the civil rights, American Indian and women's movements later in the twentieth century.

The 1910s, when Virginia women organized their most ambitious campaign for the vote, was a promising time for reformers. It was the high point of what was called the Progressive Era, when men and women, black and white, advocated prison reform and temperance, or prohibition, and formed associations to improve public education, public health, public safety and working conditions for women and children. Reformers also attacked political corruption and the increased economic and political influence of national corporations. Thousands of Virginians embraced Progressive proposals. Woman suffrage became a key objective of many Progressives. As Richmond activist Ora Brown Stokes explained to the convention of the Virginia State Federation of Colored Women's Clubs in 1921, "These are some of the problems that face us: Enforcement of child welfare laws; care of the feeble-minded; abolishment of jails and establishment of prison farms; better health laws; and police regulation of dance halls." To achieve those objectives, women needed the vote. "Let our vote be cast always," Stokes concluded, "with the one sublime purpose of making all agencies, whether political, social or otherwise, contribute their quota to the realization of our dreams of a world which has been made better by our having lived in it."[3]

Throughout Virginia's history, people—especially African Americans such as Stokes—struggled against the odds to achieve major reforms. When the woman suffrage movement began in the state early in the twentieth century, a mere half century after the Civil War, the political climate was extremely inhospitable. The Constitutional Convention of 1901–2 had undone many of the democratic reforms of the nineteenth century, including universal manhood suffrage, and severely restricted the abilities of both white and black men to register and vote. As the editor of the *St. Luke Herald*, an African American newspaper in Richmond, pointed out on the forty-ninth anniversary of the city's liberation in April 1865 by the U.S. Army, "There are those who declare that the enfranchisement of the Negro was the greatest mistake and crime of the nation. We think not so; had not the Negro been armed with the ballot his freedom would have meant nothing." The right of African American men to vote as guaranteed by the Fifteenth Amendment to the Constitution of the United States "was not a mistake," declared the editor, but "a God sent opportunity, by which the Negro showed his ability to measure up to conditions of manhood and citizenship though just out of the land of slavery." It was unfortunate for the mostly elite white women who founded the twentieth-century suffrage movement in Virginia that they did so at the lowest point of debasement of African Americans during the long Jim Crow period. Proposals to make any changes at all to suffrage legislation aroused fears that African Americans might return to politics and, as had happened briefly in Virginia late in the 1870s and early in the 1880s, form a coalition with white working-class voters and take control of state government.[4]

The story of the campaign Virginia women made for the vote during the 1910s has never been told in full and deserves to be. It was not a failure as passing references have generally characterized it. It is true that members of the all-male General Assembly defeated proposals in 1912, 1914 and 1916 to amend the Constitution of Virginia to grant women the vote, and in 1920, they refused to ratify the Nineteenth Amendment to the Constitution of the United States that achieved that objective for all American women. What most historians failed to notice, however, is that in March 1920, both houses of the General Assembly—by significant majorities—took the first step in the two-and-a-half-year process to amend the state constitution to authorize woman suffrage. The woman suffrage movement actually achieved a notable and rather surprising success in Virginia, although it was too late to make any practical difference.

This book and *We Demand: Women's Suffrage in Virginia*, the major exhibition at the Library of Virginia in 2020 to commemorate the centennial of woman suffrage in the United States and Virginia, introduce readers and visitors to some remarkable Virginia women whose names have scarcely ever appeared in any historical narrative. Dedicated, hardworking and extraordinarily capable, those women deserve recognition right alongside the heroes of the American Revolution and the civil rights movement for their work to expand democracy in the state. Their deeds are recorded in several sources.

The abundant archive of the Equal Suffrage League of Virginia and the surviving records of the Congressional Union/National Woman's Party for Virginia are preserved in the Library of Virginia. The personal papers of Adèle Clark in the library of Virginia Commonwealth University include a large quantity of suffrage materials. The personal papers of Lila Meade Valentine, in the Virginia Historical Society, and the papers of Sophie Gooding Rose Meredith, in possession of Sophie Meredith Sides Cowan of Blue Hill, Maine, and Tucson, Arizona, each contain a smaller number of suffrage records. The National American Woman Suffrage Association Papers and the National Woman's Party Papers, both in the Library of Congress, also contain valuable records of the work of Virginia suffragists. Together with the publications of suffrage organizations and the state's newspapers, those records make it possible to revise the historical narrative and document how suffragists in Virginia achieved their overlooked but admittedly limited success.

The Equal Suffrage League Records and the Congressional Union/National Woman's Party Records have been scanned and are two of the free digital collections available through the Library of Virginia's Virginia Memory website. Images and text from *We Demand: Women's Suffrage in Virginia* are included in the exhibition section of Virginia Memory. Biographies of several dozen women who worked for or against woman suffrage or who held public office in the 1920s can also be viewed on the Library of Virginia's *Dictionary of Virginia Biography* website and the online national biographical directory of woman suffrage that the Women and Social Movements in the United States project created. A full list of those biographies is in the appendix of this volume.

This account of the woman suffrage movement in Virginia is largely about the women who led the campaign, but it suggests several lines of future research that could enrich our understanding of the context and of the people who supported woman suffrage but were not leaders in the movement. For instance, we know what leaders said and did in public, but we do not know much about how people who heard them speak reacted and what aspects of their lives influenced how they heard the speakers. Those so-far voiceless women (and men, too) would have had numerous and varied experiences and outlooks that shaped their responses depending on whether they were white or African American; young, middle-aged or older; how much or what kind of education they had; whether they lived in cities, small towns or in rural areas; whether they belonged to women's clubs or service organizations; whether their churches encouraged them to engage in social service projects; whether they were single, married or widowed; whether they had children or grandchildren; whether they were wage-earners who worked outside the home; whether their husbands or fathers voted. Our knowledge about African American women's clubs and organizations through the scattered and incomplete surviving records could be substantially enhanced with diligent additional research that might discover more records.

2

NO WOMAN SOLE OR COVERT

VIRGINIA WOMEN AND THE VOTE BEFORE 1920

*V*irginia law did not authorize women to vote before ratification of the Nineteenth Amendment in 1920, but in a small number of isolated instances before that a few women did.

COLONIAL AND REVOLUTIONARY WOMEN

It is unlikely that any Virginia women voted before the American Revolution. English law, which became Virginia law, severely restricted the actions of people who were in dependent circumstances, such as children, women and indentured servants. Dependent people, even after they attained an age of informed consent, were not regarded as having sufficient independence to vote. Under the common law of coverture, a woman lost her separate legal identity when she married and became legally dependent on her husband. Unmarried women were ordinarily regarded as dependent on their fathers or other adult male relatives. They could not, therefore, by definition, be capable of voting. As a consequence, some of the common nouns used in Virginia election laws in the seventeenth and eighteenth centuries to identify people eligible to vote had what we would describe in the twenty-first century as default white adult male meanings.[1]

In July 1619, at the first election held in Virginia—to elect burgesses to serve in the General Assembly—the governor's summons directed that the burgesses be "chosen by the inhabitants" but without stating specifically which inhabitants. In 1624, the governor authorized "all freemen" in each settlement to select burgesses "by pluralitie of voices." That clearly limited voting to free males: no women, indentured servants (even if male) and certainly no children, enslaved people or Indians.[2]

Insofar as the incomplete files of early seventeenth-century laws disclose, "all freemen" could vote until 1670. An important law of that year restricted voting to "freeholders and housekeepers who only are answerable to the publique for the levies." The words *freeholders* (owners of land) and *housekeepers* (heads of household) in the 1670 law could theoretically have been interpreted to mean that some unmarried or widowed women housekeepers who owned land or paid taxes might have regarded themselves as thereby qualified, but researchers have found no evidence in the incomplete seventeenth-century records that any voted or tried to vote. In 1684, the General Assembly confined the vote to landowners—freeholders only, excluding housekeepers—and in 1699 passed a law that explicitly declared "that no woman sole or covert… be enabled to give a vote or have a voice in the election of burgesses." The legal terms *femme sole* meant an unmarried woman and *femme covert* a married woman. Perhaps some women had made an attempt to vote, or perhaps some legislators wanted to prevent them from trying. The wording of the law opens the question but does not close the door on the answer. The legislators may have been erecting a new prohibition to women voting, but they were probably reinforcing an existing common law barrier.[3]

Election laws passed in 1705 and 1736 enfranchised only freeholders who owned one hundred acres of land or fifty acres and a house for the election of members of the House of Burgesses, the only elected public officials in the colony. The laws incorporated the understanding in the 1699 act that had defined women who owned enough land as not freeholders for the purpose of voting. The state's first constitution, adopted in 1776, continued in force without modification the law of 1736 for election of members of Virginia's Senate and House of Delegates.[4]

It is possible, but not probable, that a few property-owning widowed or unmarried women voted for county tax commissioners from 1778 to 1781. Late in 1777, the General Assembly levied a tax on land and some items of personal property to be collected in each of the succeeding six years. The law authorized "the freeholders and housekeepers of each county or corporation within this commonwealth" to elect tax commissioners to assess the value of the taxable property annually. Did the inclusion of the additional phrase "and housekeepers" extend suffrage, the right to vote, for the single purpose of the election of tax commissioners to male heads of households who owned a smaller amount of property than the required minimum or to unmarried or widowed women who were heads of households?[5]

Richard Henry Lee thought that it did. He was a member of the House of Delegates when the bill passed and presumably understood the legislators' intentions. We know what he thought from the published text of a letter he wrote to his sister on March 17, 1778. Lee was responding to a complaint from his widowed sister, Hannah Lee Corbin, that her property had been overvalued for tax purposes. Unfortunately, her letter is lost. It is therefore unclear whether she may also have suggested that she should not be taxed at all because she was not represented in the General Assembly by legislators she could vote for or against as the Virginia Declaration of Rights of 1776 appeared to guarantee—taxation without representation in violation of one of the key principles of the American Revolution. What her brother wrote to her, though, has often been cited as evidence of Corbin's asking for the right of widowed women who owned property to vote for members of the General Assembly and of Lee's agreement.

However, she may have asked for less, and he definitely agreed to less. Lee explained that under the 1777 law, "commissioners are annually chosen by the freeholders and housekeepers, and in the choice of whom you have as legal a right to vote as any other person." He referred to the election of tax assessors only, not of legislators. No researcher has yet discovered that any women voted for tax commissioners before 1781 when the General Assembly changed the law and directed that county courts appoint commissioners rather than allow freeholders and householders to elect them.[6]

IN THE NINETEENTH CENTURY

On October 20, 1829, soon after Virginia's second constitutional convention first met, an unidentified person writing with the pseudonym Virginia Freewoman published a long plea in the *Richmond Enquirer* that women who owned property be allowed to vote the same as men who owned property. Not one member of the convention replied to her request or made a formal motion to that effect. In fact, they added the words *white* and *male* to Article III Section 13, the suffrage provision of the Virginia Constitution of 1830. The Virginia Constitutions of 1851 and 1864 retained that language.

Nevertheless, in May 1832, the Shenandoah Valley town of Staunton apparently allowed women who owned taxable property to record their opinions in what appears to have been an advisory referendum on whether to raise property taxes to pay for installation of a municipal water supply system. Of the 130 voters identified by name on the poll list, 8 were women. The list described them obscurely as "Proxies." The word *proxy* ordinarily signifies a person who substitutes for, or is deputized to act for and on behalf of, another person. On the poll list 8 women's names and 11 men's names appear as proxies. That suggests that even though those 19 people were not legally entitled to vote for public officials (the men perhaps because they owned too little property, the women because they were women), the town's governing council wished to obtain the opinions of all the tax-paying property owners before they decided whether to raise taxes for "Watering the Town."[7]

During the Constitutional Convention of 1867–68, federal judge John C. Underwood, who was president of the convention, proposed votes for "our female citizens" in an unusual January 16, 1868 speech from the floor of the convention. He acknowledged that "such is the prejudice of our people, and so little are we yet advanced beyond that savage state of society which makes conscientious and heaven-inspired woman the drudge or toy of her stronger and coarser companion, that I despair at this time of securing so desirable a progress." That was the first time so far as is known that any public official in Virginia publicly proposed to extend the franchise to women, but no member even put Underwood's recommendation into a formal motion. The constitutional convention, at the insistence of Congress, granted African American men the right to vote in 1869, but no member of the convention—not even the African American men—formally proposed votes for African American women, as some of those women certainly desired.[8]

Some people—mostly women—believed that the Fourteenth Amendment to the Constitution of the United States, which was ratified in 1868, declared them citizens and thereby endowed them with the fundamental right of citizenship, the right to vote. The first two sentences of the amendment are: "All persons born or naturalized in the United States and subject to the jurisdiction thereof, are citizens of the United States and of the State wherein they reside. No State shall make or enforce any law which shall abridge the privileges or immunities of citizens of the United States." The men who wrote the amendment, the congressmen and senators who voted for it and submitted it to the states, and presumably most or all the men in state legislatures who voted to ratify it did not intend the apparently clear phrase "All persons" to include women for the purpose of the franchise if voting were one of the "privileges or immunities of citizens of the United States."[9]

Nevertheless, at least one Virginia woman tried and invoked the authority of the Fourteenth Amendment. Anna Whitehead Bodeker was one of several Richmond women who published a two-part "Defence of Woman Suffrage" in the *Richmond Daily Enquirer* on March 18 and 23, 1870. On May 6, Bodeker was elected the founding president of the Virginia State Woman Suffrage Association, the earliest-known organization to promote woman suffrage in the state. Among its members were several prominent men who had been involved in political reform in the 1860s and their wives, including John C. Underwood and his wife, Maria Gloria Jackson Underwood, a cousin of Thomas J. "Stonewall" Jackson. The association brought to Virginia nationally known advocates of woman suffrage such as Susan B. Anthony to speak on behalf of woman suffrage, but the association eventually collapsed for want of enough supporters. In November 1871, Bodeker went to a polling place in Richmond to vote. When denied the right to place her ballot in the box, she placed in it instead a note declaring that according to the Fourteenth Amendment she was an American citizen and therefore had a constitutional right to vote.[10]

The phrase "All persons" in the Fourteenth Amendment also did not include American Indians, either male or female. In 1924, Congress passed the Indian Citizenship Act that declared native-born Indians citizens of the United States, which the Nationality Act of 1940 confirmed. In Virginia, however, following passage of the Racial Integrity Act of 1924, the state did not officially acknowledge the legal existence of any Indians. Whether any or many Virginia Indians paid the poll tax, registered and voted before the 1924 and 1940 federal laws is unclear. In 1954, the General Assembly amended the Racial Integrity Act to permit Indians to register and vote without paying the poll tax so as to preserve their tax-exempt status under treaties negotiated in the seventeenth century.

In 1893, Orra Henderson Moore Gray Langhorne, who lived in Lynchburg, formed the second woman suffrage organization in Virginia. Described by a relative as "a radical by instinct, and a reformer by temperament," she started to express her views on postwar reconciliation, suffrage and African American advancement soon after the Civil War. She published numerous articles in local, regional and national newspapers,

Like the woman pictured here, Anna Whitehead Bodeker, founder of the Virginia State Woman Suffrage Association, attempted to vote in Richmond in 1871. *Library of Virginia*.

and by 1881 she was writing a regular column for the *Southern Workman*, a publication of Hampton Normal and Agricultural Institute (later Hampton University). Langhorne's views on racial cooperation and educational opportunities for African Americans were progressive for the times.[11]

Langhorne twice petitioned the General Assembly for voting rights for women in presidential elections. In her 1880 petition, she also asked that the assembly take "steps to so amend the constitution as to establish the equal rights of all citizens, irrespective of sex." Langhorne revived the campaign for woman suffrage in 1893 and established the Virginia Suffrage Society (later the Virginia Suffrage Association). She was its only president, but she could not overcome organizational problems and low membership, and the organization dissolved before the end of the decade.[12]

After the demise of the Virginia Suffrage Association, Langhorne continued her suffrage advocacy as a writer, speaker and delegate to national conventions of the National American Woman Suffrage Association, which was founded in 1890 as the result of the merging of two national suffrage organizations. In her last report to the association in 1898, Langhorne remained optimistic. "There is a steady increase of progressive sentiment in the State, particularly with the young people," she wrote hopefully. Langhorne's pioneering efforts, although ultimately unsuccessful, received national recognition. She brought nationally known suffrage leaders such as Susan B. Anthony and Carrie Chapman Catt to Virginia, but ill health prevented Langhorne from active participation during the last years of her life.[13]

SOME WOMEN VOTE

The suffrage provisions of all the state's constitutions from that of 1776 through that of 1902 specified that only men were able to vote for members of the General Assembly or other public offices. That did not necessarily prohibit women from voting in other circumstances, such as in the 1832 advisory referendum in Staunton. Published research has disclosed no other such instance in the nineteenth century, but several town charters the General Assembly amended late in the century and early in the twentieth specifically allowed both qualified voters and freeholders to vote in municipal referenda to authorize towns to borrow money—so did some laws that authorized counties to contract debts to raise money for construction or maintenance of roads and bridges. The assembly also allowed both qualified voters and freeholders to vote in the 1904 ratification referendum for the first charter of the town of Madison Heights, in Amherst County. It is possible that some women freeholders may have voted in those or similar referenda, but to date no evidence has come to light that any did.

In two instances that may be unique, the General Assembly specifically permitted women property owners to vote in referenda on proposals to allow town governments to borrow money. An amendment to the Waynesboro town charter the assembly approved in 1896 required a two-thirds vote of freeholders to authorize the city to borrow money. It was clear: "Any person, male or female, twenty-one years of age, and owning real estate in the town, shall have the right to vote in such election." The provision reappeared in almost identical language in a 1904 revision of the charter. Women who owned taxable real estate in Waynesboro voted on May 9, 1911, when by a vote of 47–4 property owners approved a town council proposal to mortgage the town's school property to raise $8,000 for building a new school. Among the 51 voters, according to the *Staunton Daily*

Leader, "were many women who exercised their privilege and supported the movement for better school facilities."[14]

Women property owners also voted in two advisory referenda in the town of Falls Church in June 1915. One referendum approved the town council's proposal to increase the real estate tax rate from sixty to eighty cents for every one hundred dollars of its assessed value. The other referendum was on whether the town council should adopt and enforce an optional 1912 state law to require mandatory residential segregation by race in the state's cities and towns. Both proposals passed with the votes of some women. In 1916, the General Assembly amended the charter of Falls Church and, as in the case of Waynesboro, specifically granted the vote to all "male or female" freeholders in referenda for borrowing money.[15]

The Waynesboro and Falls Church charter amendments and elections were unusual, but without a review of every local election prior to the general election of November 1920, it is impossible to know whether the referenda were unique. A few Virginia women definitely voted before ratification of the Nineteenth Amendment. A few brief newspaper stories covered those elections, and the nationally circulated *Woman's Journal* reported on the two Falls Church referenda. For some inexplicable reason, advocates of woman suffrage in Virginia evidently did not argue or publicly point out to members of the General Assembly that if they had believed that property-owning women were sufficiently trustworthy and competent to vote on municipal debt issues they should trust women to vote for elective officials. But they did not.

WORK LIKE HELL AND EDUCATE

THE EQUAL SUFFRAGE LEAGUE OF VIRGINIA

The campaign for woman suffrage was well underway in the United States and elsewhere when Virginians formed the third state organization to win the vote for women. In 1869, Elizabeth Cady Stanton and Susan B. Anthony formed the National Woman Suffrage Association, and Lucy Stone founded the American Woman Suffrage Association. American women first won the vote in 1890 when Wyoming entered the United States with woman suffrage in its state constitution. That same year, the national suffrage organizations merged as the National American Woman Suffrage Association (often referred to as NAWSA). Colorado adopted woman suffrage in 1893; Utah and Idaho in 1896; Washington in 1910; California in 1911; and Oregon, Kansas and the new state of Arizona in 1912. In some states, women won full voting rights; in others, they had the right to vote only in some local elections or in presidential elections.

THE EQUAL SUFFRAGE LEAGUE

In two meetings on November 20 and 27, 1909, in the elegant Richmond parlor of Anne Warfield Clay Crenshaw, about twenty socially prominent women founded the Equal Suffrage League of Virginia "to secure the suffrage for women on equal terms with men" by an amendment to the state constitution. Among the founders were the nationally known novelist Ellen

Glasgow; artists Adèle Clark and Nora Houston; Sophie Gooding Rose Meredith, whose husband had been a member of the recent Constitutional Convention of 1901–2; and Lila Hardaway Meade Valentine, who was active in several educational and public health reform organizations and the wife of a prosperous Richmond businessman. The critically acclaimed and financially successful novelist Mary Johnston was probably not present at the first meeting, but she joined almost immediately and may have attended the second meeting. The members elected Valentine president, Glasgow and Meredith vice presidents, Johnston an honorary vice president and chair of the legislative committee, and Clark recording secretary. All the members of the league then and thereafter were white.[1]

League members began work immediately. With sixty-one new members by January 6, 1910, the league treasurer reported to the monthly meeting of the board of directors a donation of $2.50 "that had been held in trust" for Orra Gray Langhorne, founder in 1893 of the Virginia Suffrage Society, "which had passed out of existence." Langhorne "had requested that it be given to a Virginia Equal Suffrage League, whenever one be formed." Early in 1910, the league affiliated with the National American Woman Suffrage Association, which also favored amendments to state constitutions rather than an amendment to the Constitution of the United States.[2]

When the General Assembly of Virginia convened in its regular biennial session on January 12, 1910, officers of the league placed on the desk of every legislator a copy of Johnston's article "The Status of Woman," from the December 11, 1909 issue of the *Richmond Times-Dispatch*, and a statement endorsing woman suffrage by the president of the College of William and Mary, Dr. Lyon G. Tyler, a son of President John Tyler. During that session of the assembly, the league adopted a resolution to oppose a bill that would have weakened inspection standards for milk and also opposed a bill to relax the state law that placed a ten-hour limit on the legal workday for women. The league brought NAWSA president Anna Howard Shaw to Richmond to lecture on behalf of woman suffrage and created a weekly lecture series in Richmond at which suffragists spoke on votes for women and a variety of related topics. A delegation from the league attended the national convention of NAWSA in April. League officers also announced their intention to organize statewide.

Glasgow had been the first of the group to endorse woman suffrage publicly and eventually eclipsed Mary Johnston as the most famous woman writer in twentieth-century Virginia. She withdrew from active advocacy of the cause in Virginia following the August 1911 death of her sister

Novelist Ellen Glasgow was an enthusiastic supporter of woman suffrage and helped establish the Equal Suffrage League of Virginia in 1909. *Library of Virginia*.

Cary Glasgow McCormack, also a founder of the league, and subsequent relocation to New York. Johnston may then have been the best-known and best-paid woman writer in the United States. Her 1911 novel *The Long Roll* was at that time (and for some critics is still) regarded as among the

Novelist Mary Johnston joined the Equal Suffrage League of Virginia in 1909 and regularly spoke on behalf of suffrage throughout Virginia. *Library of Virginia.*

best Civil War fiction. Johnston wrote articles in support of woman suffrage for newspapers and for influential national journals such as "The Woman's War" in the April 1910 issue of the *Atlantic Monthly* and "The Woman Movement" in the March 15, 1913 issue of the *Woman's Journal.* Her pioneering 1913 feminist novel *Hagar,* written and published during her most active work for woman suffrage, promoted woman suffrage within her larger vision of feminism and women's rights.[3]

Until about 1916, when for personal reasons Johnston largely withdrew from public appearances, she generously lent her time and fame to the cause of woman suffrage. She took elocution lessons to improve her skill and confidence in public speaking and allowed other suffragists to exploit her celebrity and advertise her lectures on literature and her suffrage speeches as special events. Johnston traveled extensively on behalf of woman suffrage, spoke in many towns and cities in Virginia and attended state and national conferences of suffrage organizations. In 1912, she spoke in favor of woman suffrage to a conference of the nation's governors. Johnston addressed committees of both houses of the General Assembly of Virginia in January 1912 and legislators in Tennessee in January 1913, but she persuaded neither state to change its laws or constitutions to grant women the vote.

According to Virginia state librarian Henry Read McIlwaine, woman suffrage became such a popular topic of debate and discussion in clubs and societies in the state that in 1910 he compiled a list of books and periodicals on the subject for people to "fortify themselves" with before they engaged in public discussion. The league opened a reading room in its Richmond headquarters. Janetta R. FitzHugh, a socially prominent Fredericksburg advocate of public health, and another woman donated twenty-five books on public health and morality to the league's Richmond reading room in the summer of 1910.[4]

PROGRESSIVE SUFFRAGISTS

In several respects, FitzHugh was typical of Virginia's leading suffragist activists. She was white, lived in a city (even though a comparatively small one), had socially and politically prominent relatives and was engaged in several civic reform movements. FitzHugh was atypical, but far from unique, in that she never married. She believed that woman suffrage was a civic right to which she and other women were entitled as well as a potent vehicle for achieving some of the civic goals for which she worked. As early as December 1901, FitzHugh had been treasurer of the woman's committee of managers for the Mary Washington Hospital in Fredericksburg, and she later became vice president of its executive board. In 1911, she organized the founding meeting of the Fredericksburg Civic Betterment Club in the rooms of the Business Men's Association. Elected president of the club, FitzHugh focused its initial work on garbage collection and other public health matters.[5]

Like FitzHugh in Fredericksburg, most women elsewhere in Virginia who believed in woman suffrage and joined the Equal Suffrage League were involved in or supported one or more of the social reforms that during the first years of the twentieth century became known as the Progressive movement, a nationwide impulse directed at improving public education, public health, and civic life. One of Roanoke's committed suffragists, Willie Brown Walker Caldwell, had similar civic interests. She was a leader in the Woman's Civic Betterment Club, which promoted several important public health and civic improvement projects in Roanoke and led to the creation of the first public library in the city. Equal Suffrage League president Lila Meade Valentine was a founder of the Instructive Visiting Nurse Association, which provided free healthcare for poor people and led efforts that improved public schools and public education in Richmond and statewide. She also supported the work of the Southern Education Board to improve the quality of public education for African Americans and arranged for its 1903 annual convention to meet in Richmond.[6]

Throughout the nation, educational reformers, public health advocates, supporters of temperance and prohibition, and people who worked for child labor laws and juvenile justice reform perceived votes for women as a desirable new tool to obtain changes in municipal, state and national laws for the benefit of women, children and families. The woman suffrage movement united white Virginia women who were working on parallel lines for social, educational and economic reforms during the 1910s. African American women formed their own separate Progressive social reform

Lila Meade Valentine was the founding president of the Equal Suffrage League of Virginia. *VCU Libraries*.

organizations. Indeed, women were largely responsible for creating and sustaining progressive reform in Virginia early in the twentieth century. As with Valentine, FitzHugh and Caldwell, they believed or came to believe that suffrage was in itself a valuable right of citizenship.

Both the suffrage movement and the Progressive movement were for the most part inspired by and under the leadership of a large number of elite or professional white urban women. Most of the women who took leadership roles in the suffrage campaign lived in cities or large towns, and they were prosperous and socially prominent or had professional careers in education, healthcare or business. Many of them also had cooks and household servants, who were overwhelmingly African American and performed many of the time-consuming tasks that less-prosperous women had to perform for themselves, such as cooking, cleaning, washing clothes and minding children. Some women were young and unmarried, some were mothers and some were grandmothers. The married women among them nearly all had husbands who supported their engagement in civic reforms of various kinds.

Valentine's businessman husband was particularly supportive and joined the Equal Suffrage League. In a love letter to her in 1913, he summarized their shared beliefs: "I believe that in advocating the suffrage for women you are not only advocating a righteous cause but one which will aid in the relief of the weary and the heavy laden, promote patriotism in its highest sense and advance the cause of peace among the peoples. My spirit is with you in the work, beloved, and I bid you God speed."[7]

Valentine summed up her motivations with a somewhat different emphasis in a September 1916 speech to the annual convention of the National American Woman Suffrage Association to explain why she and other suffragists worked as hard as they did for votes for women. She believed in women; she was an early feminist. "If I were asked to give one reason above all others, for advocating the enfranchisement of women," Valentine began, "I should unhesitatingly reply, 'The necessity for the complete development of woman, as a prerequisite for the highest development of the race.'" By that, Valentine almost certainly meant the human race and may not have necessarily limited her vision to white people. Otherwise, however, most suffragists usually addressed themselves to the interests of white women because they saw themselves as distinct from African Americans. That constant consciousness of racial differences pervaded the culture.

"Just so long as woman remains under guardianship, as if she were a minor or an incompetent," Valentine explained, "just so long as she passively accepts at the hands of men, conditions, usages, laws, as if they were decrees of Providence—just so long as she is deprived of the educative responsibilities of self government—by just so much does she fall short of complete development, as a human being, and by just so much does she retard the progress of the race."

Valentine continued, "We are the children of our mothers as well as of our fathers. We inherit the defects as well as the perfections of both. Many a man goes down in his profession—is a 'failure in life,' as the phrase goes, because, forsooth, he is the son of an undeveloped mother, and like her, is lacking in independence, in initiative, in the ability to seize upon golden opportunities. Yet she was trained to passivity, to submission, to the obliteration of whatever personality she may once have possessed. What more could we expect of her son?" Valentine pronounced the suffrage movement, "with all that it implies of freedom for self-development and equality of opportunity…a clarion call to the woman of today. It bids her stand up and think for herself; and equipping her with the new tool of democracy, it urges her to assume the responsibilities of a full grown human being, and to take her share in the making of the world about her."[8]

Business and professional women were also active in the suffrage movement. The best known of them, Ellen Gertrude Tompkins Kidd, of Richmond, was a nationally, even internationally, recognized business leader when she was elected treasurer of the Equal Suffrage League in 1910. Her Pin Money Pickle Company, which she had founded shortly after the Civil War and continued to direct, had grown into an international business with a large pickling plant in Richmond. Leading hotels throughout the United States featured her pickles by name on their menus, as did dining cars on many of the rail lines in the country. She also sold pickles abroad. Kidd was treasurer of the league from 1910 until the campaign for votes for women was won in 1920.[9]

Richmond artists Adèle Clark and Nora Houston (pronounced House-ton) worked for woman suffrage throughout the decade. Both studied art in New York, taught at the Art Club of Richmond and, about 1916, established their own studio, the Atelier. Clark, a painter primarily of portraits, landscapes and religious scenes, exhibited canvases at the Carnegie Institute in Pittsburgh and at Richmond's Valentine Museum. Her life exemplified the crucial role women played in the social reform movements of the twentieth century. She applied her sharp intellect, artistic skills and determination to champion women and the arts. Clark was more prominent as an art teacher than as an artist and was a leading advocate for women's rights for six decades, beginning with her role in the founding of the Equal Suffrage League.[10]

Right: Ellen Tompkins Kidd of Richmond, founder of the Pin Money Pickle Company, was treasurer of the Equal Suffrage League of Virginia. *Library of Virginia.*

Below: Members of the Equal Suffrage League of Virginia (*clockwise from left*) Nora Houston, Eugenia Jobson, Mae Schaill and Adèle Clark, about 1915. *VCU Libraries.*

Houston's academic background in the classical elements of painting plus her exposure to newer influences were reflected in her art. Her works included portraits, landscapes of the Virginia countryside and paintings of African American neighborhoods and everyday life. Houston's residence in New York and abroad not only elevated her training as an artist but also exposed her to social and cultural changes taking place early in the twentieth century. Witnessing various forms of social injustice experienced by the poor and working class influenced both her art and her development as an activist. Houston served as recording secretary for the Equal Suffrage League of Richmond from 1914 to 1919 and worked diligently throughout the state giving lectures, developing local chapters and lobbying state legislators. She frequently spoke on street corners and parks in Richmond and at least once had rocks thrown at her, one of which she kept until her death.[11]

Women who worked for better conditions for other women and for children also joined the movement for woman suffrage. For instance, Clark's sister Edith Clark Cowles, although living in New York in 1909, may have attended some preliminary meetings in Richmond that led to the founding of the Equal Suffrage League. After Cowles moved back to Virginia with her children early in the 1910s, she frequently wrote letters to Virginia newspapers on topics that interested her, including women's rights. In 1917, Cowles responded to an editorial about medical universities opening their doors to women in which the editor had expressed surprise that women could handle the rigors of medical school. Cowles explained that women could, indeed, study medicine, but that in the past they had been "stilted in the development of their inherent power…due to the many centuries in which men have excluded them from educational, economic and political equality." Cowles also contributed regularly to the syndicated newspaper column "Training Little Children," which reached a nationwide audience.[12]

Suffragist Fannie Stratton Bayly King was one of the most influential women in Staunton. She had been active for more than a decade in community improvement projects and organizations, including the women's auxiliary of the YMCA. Early in the twentieth century, King was president of the local branch of the Co-Operative Education Association that worked (sometimes across racial and social class lines) to improve public education. She was also active in the Staunton Civic Club, a member of both women's clubs in the city, a supporter of the public health work of the Instructive Visiting Nurse Association and vice president of the Virginia Library Association. The 1912 state convention of the Virginia Federation of Women's Clubs,

Fannie Bayly King, president of the Equal Suffrage League of Staunton. *Staunton Public Library*.

which met in Staunton when King was the federation's president, refused to endorse woman suffrage. The federation's leaders badly disappointed her.[13]

Woman suffrage advocate Agnes Dillon Randolph was a Richmond nurse who from 1900 to 1904 and again from 1910 to 1913 was superintendent of the Richmond Virginia Hospital Training School for Nurses. She then

Mrs. KATE WALLER BARRETT,

GENERAL SUPERINTENDENT OF NATIONAL FLORENCE CRITTENTON MISSION,
218 THIRD STREET N.W., WASHINGTON, D. C.

Dr. Kate Waller Barrett, founding president of the Equal Suffrage League of Alexandria. *Library of Virginia.*

became superintendent of nurses at Richmond's Memorial Hospital but in 1914 had to step down in favor of a male superintendent. Randolph was executive secretary of the Virginia Anti-Tuberculosis League from 1914 to 1919 and directed a comprehensive tuberculosis survey of Norfolk County in 1917, the first ever in that part of Virginia. During that work, she became well known at the state capitol for her advocacy of public health measures, including proper treatment for African American tubercular patients.[14]

Dr. Katherine Harwood Waller Barrett, of Alexandria, was also an active suffragist. One of the few licensed female medical doctors in the state, she was president of the National Florence Crittenton Mission, the first national philanthropic institution with a congressional charter. The mission's primary goal was the welfare of unmarried mothers, and its work on behalf of women and children became nationally known, as did she. In 1911, Barrett was elected president of the National Council of Women, an affiliate of the International Council of Women, which suffrage advocates Elizabeth Cady Stanton and Susan B. Anthony founded in the nineteenth century.[15]

Lillie Mary Barbour also was an early suffragist. She lived and worked in Roanoke, where she joined the Local Union No. 48 of the United Garment Workers of America. She was secretary of the union and was often a delegate to the annual meetings of the Virginia Federation of Labor. Barbour embraced the cause of woman suffrage and spoke to unions about the importance of woman suffrage in the campaign to obtain better working conditions. She also addressed suffrage meetings around the state about labor issues related to women and children and argued that "the ballot in our hands is the only thing to help us." In 1917, Barbour was reportedly instrumental in securing the Virginia Federation of Labor's endorsement of woman suffrage at its state convention. Believing that education could also help improve conditions for working women, she supported the efforts of the

Co-Ordinate College League of Virginia to establish a women's college at the University of Virginia.[16]

Edmonia Carter Powers Barksdale, of Richmond and Albemarle County, assisted philanthropist Grace Evelyn Arents in establishing a country retreat for the working women of Richmond in the 1880s. Barksdale was one of the incorporators in 1901 of the Co-Operative Workers of Richmond, which managed its retreat, Summer Rest, in Albemarle County and directed it for several years. She was active in the Society for the Prevention of Cruelty to Animals and was president in 1902 of the Consumers' League of Richmond. Barksdale was a founding member of the Equal Suffrage League and in 1913 was president of the Equal Suffrage League of Greenwood, in Albemarle County. At age sixty-seven in February 1914, she was the oldest of the suffragists who addressed the Committee on Privileges and Elections of the House of Delegates. No text of her address survives, but newspaper reports indicated that she was blunt in her advocacy. Two Richmond newspapers reported in identical language that Barksdale "said that after the war"—meaning the Civil War—"she had recommended the carrying of firearms by girls as a measure of self-protection in lawless times. The women of this day needed the ballot as the women of that day needed the bullet, she claimed, for their own protection."[17]

Lucy Randolph Mason, early in a long career as an advocate for working men and women in southern industry, joined the Equal Suffrage League in January 1911 because, as she explained to Lila Meade Valentine, "no life is worth the living which has not for its aim and object, not only the attainment of its own highest potentiality, but the steadfast determination to aid with its utmost endeavors in the uplifting of mankind.…When the ballot for women is presented to me as a potent agency in the divine plan for the growth and perfection of humanity on this earth, I feel that I have no right to let less important considerations make me reject what I believe to be for the best and highest interests of our future, here and hereafter."[18]

NETWORKS OF SUFFRAGISTS

Suffragists had many ways of making connections with like-minded women in other communities. Through educational and public health reform organizations, church groups, patriotic and preservation associations such as the Daughters of the American Revolution, the United Daughters of the

Ellie Putney, president of the Equal Suffrage League of Wytheville. *Courtesy of Laura Putney Wright.*

Confederacy, the Association for the Preservation of Virginia Antiquities (later Preservation Virginia) and others they had networks and membership lists by which they could identify likely partners throughout the state. The Virginia Federation of Women's Clubs, which was founded in 1907, also linked women together through their memberships in local women's clubs, many of which actively promoted educational, public health and other civic reforms in their communities.

Women's clubs were a critical nexus for suffragists to make contact with one another, both within communities and throughout the state. Betty Ellison "Ellie" Withers Putney, for example, who moved from Richmond to Wytheville early in the campaign for the vote, reported from her new home early in 1912, "We have just organized a Womans Club here & by May expect to have 15 members, it is from this membership that I am hoping to form an Equal Suffrage League here <u>but</u> it is not wise to do it until we get the Club on a fine footing....My idea is <u>not</u> to have the League a part of Club work but I will come in touch with many women I have not known before, but who being bread winners will be good material to work with."[19]

Women's clubs were not always helpful, however. Individual club leaders in some cities opposed woman suffrage, the leadership of the state federation did not endorse votes for women until June 1919 and some clubs such as the Woman's Club of Richmond had standing rules against discussion of controversial current political topics. The leaders of the club in Roanoke repeatedly refused to permit members who advocated woman suffrage to invite suffrage speakers. As late as the spring of 1919, suffragists in Roanoke were still having difficulty getting around obstructions that leaders of the woman's club there placed in the way of having woman suffrage discussed at its meetings. Sallie J. Miles, who lived in Roanoke, reported that Willie Caldwell, "who knows the Federation, thinks the majority of clubs and club members are in favor." Miles explained to Valentine, "but you know the Federation is in the hands of a few anti suffragists who dead lock everything."[20]

Elizabeth Lewis, founding president of the Equal Suffrage League of Lynchburg and longtime vice president of the Equal Suffrage League of Virginia, circa 1888. *Lynchburg Museum System.*

Members of elite Virginia families also had relatives with whom they could form alliances and recruit members. League president Lila Meade Valentine was related to lifelong Lynchburg resident Elizabeth Dabney Langhorne Lewis, a niece of Orra Gray Langhorne, who had founded a short-lived woman suffrage association in the 1890s. Lewis was herself an aunt of Nancy Witcher Langhorne Shaw Astor, Viscountess Astor, the Virginia native who was the first woman to serve in the British House of Commons. Lewis was well read, cultured, a fine pianist and an active participant in the lively musical and artistic life of Lynchburg. Although raised in the Episcopal Church, she became a Unitarian and reportedly was the first organist in the city's Unitarian Church. The widow of a successful lawyer and Confederate veteran, Lewis had a lifelong interest in education, promoted a free night school in Lynchburg and supported the efforts of Mary-Cooke Branch Munford and others to establish a college for women at the University of Virginia. Lewis belonged to the Woman's Christian Temperance Union and served twice as president of the Lynchburg Woman's Club and once as president of a local musical society. In a "Confession of Faith" Lewis published in *Virginia Suffrage News* in November 1914, she explained that "woman's qualification for citizenship is as valid as the man's—that her identity of interest, her intelligence, her morality, her patriotism and her proven efficiency" entitled women to all the rights and responsibilities of citizenship, among which "equal suffrage is an indispensable element."[21]

The abundant surviving correspondence between Valentine and Lewis, most of which is preserved with the records of the Equal Suffrage League, is rich in detail about the work they and other suffragists did during the 1910s. Each of them spent many hours almost every week for the entire decade reading and writing long and often thoughtful letters and reports. Almost all of Lewis's letters are handwritten and required long periods of time to write. Most of Valentine's are, too, although Valentine sometimes dictated to a secretary in league headquarters who typed and mailed them. Their letters also exhibit almost the only instance in which women routinely addressed each other by their given names—Dear Lila; Dear Cousin Lizzie—rather than by the formal style that women then almost universally employed—Dear Mrs. B.B. Valentine; Dear Mrs. John H. Lewis; Dear Miss FitzHugh.

SUFFRAGISTS AT WORK

The Equal Suffrage League of Virginia held its first state convention in Richmond on December 16, 1910. During 1911, the members devoted most of their energies to collecting signatures on suffrage petitions for submission to the General Assembly the following year and sponsoring public meetings at which league leaders or visiting speakers from elsewhere in the United States advocated votes for women. For instance, at the invitation of the league, noted writer Charlotte Perkins Gilman lectured at the Mechanics' Institute in Richmond in January, only one of many lectures Sophie Meredith, as a vice president and chair of the committee on lectures and literature, helped arrange. Valentine and Mary Johnston addressed the Richmond Central Trade Union Council in February and obtained its endorsement for woman suffrage. Representatives of the league and the Woman's Christian

Temperance Union held a joint meeting in Richmond on October 2. Two weeks later, Valentine hosted the organizational meeting of the Men's Equal Suffrage League of Virginia in her home, and later that month half a dozen league members attended the national convention of the National American Woman Suffrage Association in Louisville. On November 2, 1911, the league formally dedicated its second state headquarters.

Several suffragists founded local equal suffrage leagues. Valentine and her friends formed the Equal Suffrage League of Richmond, and Elizabeth Lewis and six other women formed the Equal Suffrage League of Lynchburg in October 1910. Anna Howard Shaw, president of the National American Woman Suffrage Association, joined Valentine and Johnston in Norfolk on November 18, 1910, when they and Louise Collier Willcox spoke at the organizational meeting of the Equal Suffrage League of Norfolk. Almost forgotten a century later, Willcox was then a nationally known poet, writer, editor and translator. A Chicago native, she was educated by private tutors in England, France and Germany and studied music at the Conservatory of Leipzig in 1882 and 1883. Her brother, Hiram Price, became a popular Unitarian minister in Brooklyn, New York, and later a noted writer. After she married a Virginia lawyer, she moved from New York to Norfolk.

Willcox raised a daughter and a son while writing essays, columns, criticism and verse on a very wide variety of topics for various national magazines, among them *Harper's Weekly*, *Harper's Bazaar* and the *North American Review*, and for fifteen years she was a manuscript reader for several major book publishing companies. She published several volumes of essays and poetry between 1909 and 1924. Willcox and her brother helped her friend Ellen Glasgow publish her first novel in 1897, and she and Glasgow traveled to England together in 1914. In Willcox's final *Harper's Weekly* column in August 1913, she complained that she had not been permitted to write about what she regarded as "the greatest revolution that civilization has ever seen…the emancipation of woman." She argued, "Women must be so placed as to make free and unhampered choices in all lines of life, political, economic, domestic, occupational, before we can expect a true and normal development from them" and for their daughters and sons.[22]

Forty women formed the Equal Suffrage League of Norfolk and elected Pauline Forstall Colclough Adams president. A native of Ireland, she had played a prominent role in the women's auxiliary for the 1907 exposition in Norfolk that commemorated the founding of the Virginia colony three centuries earlier, and she was a member of the Housewives' League in the city. Twenty-one people founded the Equal Suffrage League of Williamsburg

Left: Louise Collier Willcox, a Norfolk writer who supported woman suffrage, pictured here in the 1890s. *Louise Collier Willcox Papers, Albert and Shirley Small Special Collections Library, University of Virginia.*

Right: Pauline Adams, founding president of the Equal Suffrage League of Norfolk. *Library of Virginia.*

in March 1911. Its first president was Anne Baker Tucker Tyler, wife of Lyon G. Tyler, whom local suffragists boasted was the first man in the state to speak publicly on behalf of votes for women. Twenty-four women formed a league in the Richmond suburb of Highland Springs on November 1, 1911, and after Valentine and Johnston spoke in Roanoke on November 30, thirty-five women formed the Equal Suffrage League of Roanoke.[23]

Speaking on woman suffrage to varied audiences was a vitally important part of suffragists' work. Johnston and other members of the league spoke to labor groups in Newport News, Alexandria and Richmond during the spring of 1912, and Johnston and Valentine spoke together about labor and suffrage in Harrisonburg in May. Lewis and her daughter represented the

Equal Suffrage League at the annual convention of the Virginia Federation of Labor in Danville in June. Throughout the decade, the federation welcomed suffrage advocates and endorsed woman suffrage more than once.

Johnston's and Valentine's joint and separate lectures on woman suffrage made deep impressions on members of their audiences. "I do quite distinctly remember the splendid talk Mrs. Valentine made" in the West Virginia border town of Graham (later renamed Bluefield), Laura Davenport recalled more than two decades later. "She spoke from an open top Ford car. The whole thing was an innovation of course which drew a good crowd especially men with sprinkling of women. I also recall, with a smile, that after much persuasion the mayor of Graham at that time and an anti"—that is, an opponent of woman suffrage—"but a very fine and popular man, introduced Mrs. Valentine. We were much elated with this and the whole affair."[24]

OPPOSITION TO WOMAN SUFFRAGE

The idea of women voting was new to nearly all Virginians, both male and female. To many of them, it appeared to be a dangerous undermining of long-established understandings about gender roles in society and the special role people understood mothers should exercise in raising children. That is why suffragists, as Lila Meade Valentine did in her 1916 speech and in innumerable other presentations, stressed the importance of full citizenship rights for women, for mothers who raised sons into men. Some people who opposed woman suffrage believed and argued that the interests of husbands, wives and children were so intimately intertwined that men naturally represented the interests of women and their families and that therefore women did not need the vote. Other people declared that refined ladies should not descend from the lofty pedestal on which gentlemen had placed them and sully themselves by participating in the sordid business of politics. Throughout the decade, politicians often stated that they opposed woman suffrage because they believed that most Virginia women did not wish to vote. Whether they all believed that or timidly sidestepped a commitment with that as an excuse is not in every instance clearly evident.

Woman suffrage faced strong opposition from nearly every quarter throughout the decade, including from other women. When Equal Suffrage League officers addressed legislators in January 1912 on behalf of votes for women, anti-suffrage women presented a petition in opposition. The signatories included wage earners; schoolteachers; college graduates; presidents of influential women's social, literary, patriotic and charitable societies; church and missionary associations; and professional women who worked in day nurseries, orphan asylums and hospitals. Noting that women had for decades indirectly participated in the political sphere through their influence on their husbands, fathers, brothers and sons, the petition asserted "that we are convinced that a body of intelligent, capable and conscientious persons, bound by no party ties, divided by no factional disputes, and far above all suspicion of self-interest, is of infinite value to any country or State. We ask of you nothing but the continuance of our political independence."[25]

Two women in rural Carroll County on the North Carolina border proposed to discuss woman suffrage "before the people in a debate at a school entertainment," but one of them reported later that people treated their proposal "as a huge joke." In 1911, the newspaper in Fredericksburg described the city as then "the most conservative town in the South" on the subject of woman suffrage. Ellie Putney complained from Wytheville that "this is such a conservative little corner of a most conservative state" that recruiting members and persuading skeptics was difficult. In 1913, Staunton league president Mary S. Yost described her hometown as "one of the old conservative kind" with very few people willing to support votes for women. "I am surprised that we have a League at all."[26]

Staunton resident Fannie King remembered years later that after she made an address there on behalf of woman suffrage at the Working Men's Fraternal Association, whose members received her politely and complimented her on her persuasive presentation, "my male relatives and friends crossed the street or dodged into stores to keep from speaking to such a bold bad woman!!!" Indeed, "I made myself exceedingly unpopular among the 'wimmin-folks' who thought the men 'ought to manage politics.'" At the Equal Suffrage League state convention in December 1915, King accompanied a large number of delegates who called on Governor Henry Carter Stuart to urge him to endorse woman suffrage. In a widely reported exchange, King seized an opportunity to display her quick wit. When it came her turn to speak, she began, "I come from a stronghold of democracy," meaning a stronghold of the Democratic Party in the Shenandoah Valley. The governor interrupted, "Not a very recent one," referring to a Republican Party victory in the district. King retorted, "You have anticipated what I was going to say. I was going to suggest that perhaps the reason for democracy's defeat there has been the failure of its advocates to advance the principles of democracy in their fullest sense," by which she meant extending the vote to women.[27]

THE VIRGINIA ASSOCIATION
OPPOSED TO WOMAN SUFFRAGE

In March 1912, the Virginia Association of Conservative Women formed to oppose woman suffrage. It soon renamed itself the Virginia Association Opposed to Woman Suffrage. Prominent Richmond resident Jane Meade Rutherfoord was the founding president. She had been a founder of the Woman's Club of Richmond in 1894 and served twice as its president and twice as a vice president. Active in its affairs for twenty-five years, Rutherfoord worked with Lila Meade Valentine, another club member and a distant relative, in the Richmond Education Association and was an advocate for improved educational opportunities for women, including higher education. Because working-class women and some widows had to be "bread-winners," Rutherfoord stated in her 1904 presidential address to the Woman's Club, "let the stumbling blocks be removed, and every avenue be open to them which will lead to their ultimate success." Rutherfoord and Valentine shared several objectives, but Rutherfoord differed from her in believing that women and men had separate roles in society, with men responsible for public affairs and women responsible for families. Hence, her opposition to woman suffrage. Rutherfoord served as president of the association until 1915, when she was in her mid-seventies.[28]

The officers and board of directors of the Virginia Association Opposed to Woman Suffrage included women from politically influential and socially prominent families. The association's letterhead stationery featured the names of an advisory committee of more than two dozen equally prominent men. (The Equal Suffrage League letterhead did not list any men in any capacity.) No organizational records survive, but a few newspaper stories indicated that the association had about 1,900 members in December 1913, and at the May 1918 state convention officers reported on the addition of almost 1,350 new members. Insofar as the meager membership data disclose, it appears that Virginia women who joined the association and other women who opposed woman suffrage were less likely to be engaged in Progressive social reform movements than women who advocated woman suffrage.

The association's second president, Mary Mason Anderson Williams, was the daughter of a wealthy Richmond industrialist and the wife of a prosperous Richmond businessman. She later played an important role in establishing the first short-lived symphony orchestra in Richmond and was active in garden club work, but she did not participate in any of the reform organizations that engaged Richmond suffragists. Williams's main

Anti-Suffrage Arguments

Votes cannot make work when there is no work.

Votes cannot increase wages when there is no natural increase in business.

The best safeguards for the working women are found in those States where the laws have been made by men voters.

In the City of New York, if any man fails to pay the wages due a female employee up to $50.00, he is liable to be imprisoned and kept in close confinement without the privilege of bail.

In 1897 it was provided that every female operative in a factory should be given a chair to sit on at reasonable times, and in 1900 this was extended to include hotel and restaurant waitresses.

The badge of the Consumer's League has done more for the relief of the working women, than any vote could ever do.

A woman's citizenship is as great and as real as that of any man. The **Anti-Suffragists** stand for the **true** view of woman's place in the State.

**Virginia Association Opposed
To Woman Suffrage.**

Opponents distributed broadsides and other literature arguing against the vote for women. *Library of Virginia.*

focus was on historic preservation, including preservation of the culture that elite white males dominated and in which she had always lived. She was a member of the United Daughters of the Confederacy and the Confederate Memorial Literary Society, which at that time promoted reverence for the cause lost in the Civil War and looked backward rather than forward. She served for several years on the board of directors of the Association for the Preservation of Virginia Antiquities (later Preservation Virginia). At that time, it industriously promoted an interpretation of Virginia history that exalted the roles elite white men had played in the founding of the colony and nation; ignored the contributions of American Indians, African Americans and women to the colony and state; and opposed the extension of democracy that had begun with universal white manhood suffrage before the Civil War and the granting of the vote to African American men afterward. It doubtless pleased Williams very much that in July 1915, Mary Custis Lee, only living child of Confederate general Robert E. Lee, joined the Virginia Association Opposed to Woman Suffrage.[29]

The leading Virginia women who opposed woman suffrage did not subscribe to an old nineteenth-century belief that women should not take part in public affairs or speak in public. Many of them spoke out forcefully. A good example was the popular writer Molly Elliot Seawell (pronounced Sea-well), a nationally known Virginia native who took an active part in opposing woman suffrage from her home in Washington, D.C. She was deeply committed to the privileged place women of high social status had occupied in Gloucester County, where she was born in 1853 and grew up. Seawell published a controversial article in the November 28, 1891 issue of *The Critic, A Weekly Review of Literature and the Arts* titled "On the Absence of the Creative Faculty in Women." She admitted that many women writers and artists had created works of good quality, but she insisted that "no woman has ever done anything in the intellectual world, which has had the germ of immortality" and that in every field of endeavor the faculty of genius belonged exclusively to men. Although a successful writer with a long public career, including commenting on public affairs, she accepted and was comfortable with women playing subordinate roles to men in society.[30]

In April 1911, Seawell published a 119-page booklet titled *The Ladies' Battle* that opponents of woman suffrage used as a textbook and source for condemning suffragists. Early in 1912, she published two long anti-suffrage articles in the *Richmond Times-Dispatch*: "Why Women Should Not Vote" on February 25, and "Some Problems of Woman's Suffrage" on March 10, that repeated arguments

MOLLY ELLIOT SEAWELL.

Molly Elliot Seawell, a native of Gloucester County, was a nationally known writer who published anti-suffragist books and articles. *Library of Virginia.*

in *The Ladies' Battle*. Seawell stated that in each of the western states that had granted women the vote, women paid higher taxes; could be forced to support unsuccessful husbands; endured higher rates of illiteracy, poverty and divorce; were victims of more violence; and were exposed to rampant socialism and saloonkeepers' influence in politics. She also hinted that woman suffrage could lead to a dangerous return of African American voting. Seawell extended her critique to other countries and condemned militant English suffragists such as Emmeline Pankhurst, whom she characterized as a serial criminal.

Richmond artist and Equal Suffrage League founder Adèle Clark responded to Seawell's first essay in the same newspaper on March 11. Clark vigorously contradicted Seawell's numerous assertions or statements of fact and the several premises on which she had grounded her remarks. The Equal Suffrage League of Virginia published Clark's reply to Seawell as a pamphlet, *Facts vs. Fallacies: Anti-Suffrage Allegations Refuted*. Seawell remained undaunted and early in 1914 published a long article titled "Two Suffrage Mistakes" in the influential national journal *North American Review* that contained many of the same arguments as in *The Ladies' Battle*.[31]

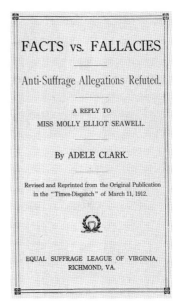

The Equal Suffrage League of Virginia published Adèle Clark's *Facts vs. Fallacies* in 1912 to refute Seawell's arguments against suffrage. *Library of Virginia.*

THE ISSUE OF RACE

Just below the surface of Seawell's objections to woman suffrage (and right on the surface of many other opponents' arguments) was a fear that animated opposition to woman suffrage throughout the states of the former Confederacy, that any expansion of suffrage could endanger the widespread disfranchisement of African Americans that those states had recently imposed, concluding with the promulgation of a new Virginia constitution in the summer of 1902.

Southern suffragists recognized and faced the problem that the issue of African American voting presented. Late in 1913, some of them formed the Southern States Woman's Suffrage Conference to combat charges that woman suffrage would lead to widespread African American voting. Some Virginia suffragists joined, although membership lists and organizational records do not survive to indicate who or how many. The Equal Suffrage League hosted the conference's second annual convention in Richmond from December 11 to 13, 1915. The conference disbanded in 1917, but the entanglement of race, gender roles and woman suffrage remained a major threat to votes for women in Virginia. Mary Johnston was a vice president but later withdrew her support because she was uneasy with the blatant racism of the conference's president, Kate Gordon of Louisiana. The letterhead of the conference stationery featured one of several maps of the United States created during the campaign for the vote that showed states with woman suffrage in white and states without in black. The legend below the map on the stationery includes a double entendre, perhaps deliberately, perhaps inadvertently: "Make the Southern States White."

Insofar as the public and private remarks of most Virginia suffragists disclose, they did not challenge or often doubt the wisdom of racial segregation and white supremacy. None of the Virginia leaders was as openly racist as Kate Gordon, but they differed among themselves about whether or how much a successful campaign for woman suffrage would lead to an enlarged number of African American voters and whether that was a genuine problem or merely a political obstacle to their main objective. When leaders of the Equal Suffrage League sought to reassure doubters, they presented their arguments in unemotional terms and with evidence that woman suffrage would considerably increase the number of white people able to vote in Virginia without dangerously increasing the number of black voters. An element of social snobbery influenced many of the league's leaders. They were willing for the small number of cultured, educated African American women to vote if they could qualify, but some of them were less willing for uncultured, uneducated men or women, black or white, to vote.[32]

The suffrage provisions in the Virginia Constitution of 1902 and the enabling acts passed in 1903 and 1904 had created a complex and prolonged process for voter registration to discourage or prevent African Americans and poor white men from voting. Men had to pay a poll tax several months before the deadline for registration and then register several months before the election. The $1.50 annual poll tax seemed small, but in fact, it was a

The letterhead of the Southern States Woman's Suffrage Conference declared its intention to protect white supremacy. *Library of Virginia.*

significant sum for many people, and it had to be paid in full for each of the three years preceding an election. In 1910, the average income in the United States has been estimated at about $700.00 a year, but people who worked in factories or in service industries usually made much less than the national average. Farmers (rural Virginians were more than half the state's total population), including both paid agricultural laborers and people who farmed their own land, earned about half the national average. People in the southern states on the whole earned about two-thirds of the national average, and most African American families in the South probably had lower annual incomes than white families. Therefore, $1.50 (or $4.50 if a person had fallen into arrears) represented a significant portion of a person's or family's income, perhaps as much as 1 or 2 percent of annual income.

Aspiring voters had to find the local tax collector and voluntarily pay the tax because the state constitution prohibited the government from actively collecting or enforcing payment of the tax. Tax collectors and voter registrars (all the registrars were partisan Democrats) had wide leeway to obstruct registration by African Americans, Republicans and anybody else they deemed politically unreliable or dangerous, which could include men who supported woman suffrage. The effect of the constitution had been to reduce the number of white men who voted by about half and to eliminate from the suffrage about 90 percent of the few African American men who had still voted in 1900. The number of Virginians who voted in the 1904 presidential election, the first statewide election after the new constitution went into effect, was scarcely half the number who had voted in 1900, the last statewide election before the constitutional convention met. During the

Virginia Warns Her People Against Woman Suffrage

TWENTY-NINE COUNTIES WOULD GO UNDER NEGRO RULE
OVER SIXTY COUNTIES IN THE STATE OF GEORGIA
THE ENTIRE STATE OF MISSISSIPPI

WHAT OF YOUR STATE, YOUR COUNTY? ISN'T IT ABOUT TIME FOR REFLECTING MEN AND WOMEN TO THINK—AND ACT?

THE THREATENED COUNTIES

From the Richmond Evening Journal May 4, 1915—Republished by Request

Several times The Richmond Evening Journal has been asked to say which counties of Virginia have more colored than white female inhabitants. The question, of course, is in connection with the somewhat noisy demands we read of in the newspapers for "votes for women." Here is the list, from the United States census of 1910:

	Colored Females.	White Females.
Amelia	2,658	1,578
Brunswick	5,549	3,843
Buckingham	3,881	3,738
Caroline	4,314	3,934
Charles City	1,817	645
Charlotte	4,267	3,599
Cumberland	2,966	1,604
Dinwiddie	4,619	2,866
Essex	2,618	1,868
Goochland	2,585	1,914
Greenesville	3,720	2,177
Halifax	10,330	9,815
Isle of Wight	3,720	3,633
King and Queen	2,635	2,069
King William	2,409	1,698
Lancaster	2,531	2,279
Lunenburg	3,338	2,856
Mecklenburg	8,280	6,160
Middlesex	2,148	2,053
Nansemond	7,847	5,602
New Kent	1,317	802
Norfolk	15,936	10,039
Northampton	4,587	3,536
Nottoway	3,715	3,016
Powhatan	1,818	1,168
Prince Edward	4,367	2,905
Prince George	2,257	1,601
Princess Anne	2,883	2,683
Southampton	8,005	5,001
Surry	2,804	1,763
Sussex	4,458	2,270
Warwick	2,053	819
Westmoreland	2,279	2,193

In Buckingham, Halifax, Lancaster and Princess Anne the whites would have a fighting chance if their women vote and present white male vote combined solidly against the colored woman and present colored male vote.

It is to be remembered that the literacy test would not work in choking off the colored woman vote. The colored people are decreasing their percentage of illiteracy very fast, especially among their women and girls. The ladies of the suffrage league will hardly come forward with a property test. No safeguard would be left but the poll tax; and if colored women knew they could get votes and rule some very rich and important counties by paying $1.50 apiece, we are inclined to think most of them would be willing to go hungry, if necessary to do it.

Probably the ladies engaged in this suffrage movement are not very practical or very logical or very well informed or disposed to bother their heads with the actual facts of politics. Most of them, we surmise, hold the somewhat vague, but firmly established feminine line of reasoning that when they want something, or think they want it, they ought to have it by all principles of wisdom and justice; and are prepared always to fall back on the traditional conclusive feminine argument "because."

No other argument, however profound, is quite so convincing or fascinating as that word "because," accompanied by some pouting of alluring and scarlet lips—especially if there be dimples by way of re-enforcement. But men are compelled and accustomed to face and deal with hard facts when considering important affairs in business or in politics. It is a hard fact that twenty-nine counties of Virginia would be condemned by woman suffrage to colored rule and five others would be in serious peril of it with woman suffrage.

We do not suppose, or imagine, that the suf-

Anti-suffragists published population figures of selected counties to suggest that woman suffrage would increase African American voting and office holding in Virginia. *Library of Virginia.*

first half of the twentieth century, a smaller proportion of all adults voted in Virginia than in any other state in the country or in any other country in the world that had or pretended to have a representative government.[33]

In 1915, Attorney General John Garland Pollard—he supported woman suffrage, and his sister Mary Ellen Pollard Clarke then worked in the Equal Suffrage League headquarters in Richmond—advised Lila Meade Valentine how to rebut charges that woman suffrage would lead to a dangerous level of black voting or office holding. He had been a member of the Constitutional Convention of 1901–2 and knew what he was talking about. Pollard pointed out to Valentine, and Valentine in turn informed other suffragists that the Constitution of 1902 allowed the General Assembly to impose a stiff property qualification for the suffrage in any city, town, county or subdivision thereof for the purpose of reducing the number of men who could vote so that no African Americans could win election to public office even in jurisdictions in which African Americans were in the majority. As Valentine often pointed out when speaking for woman suffrage or tutoring other speakers, the registration process was so difficult that white Virginians need not fear that adoption of woman suffrage would enable a larger number of African American women to register and vote than the small number of African American men who had been able to register and vote.[34]

The issues of woman suffrage and race became entangled in numerous and sometimes unpredictable ways. One was even comical. In 1913, Richmond's *News Leader*, the main afternoon daily paper in the capital, offered a prize for the best essay opposing woman suffrage. The paper received 625 essays and prepared to award the prize to Nannie Goode of Boydton, but it never did. After the editors requested a photograph of Goode for publication with the announcement of the award, they received a photograph of an African American woman and silently killed the project. The episode indicated that among influential white men, opposition to woman suffrage was strong and opposition to African American suffrage was stronger, but opposition to African Americans engaging meaningfully in public dialogue on important subjects was even stronger.[35]

AFRICAN AMERICANS AND WOMAN SUFFRAGE

African American women followed the public discussions of race and woman suffrage, and in some states woman suffrage organizations had

African American members or affiliates. The *St. Luke Herald*, whose managing editor was Richmond businesswoman and civic leader Maggie Lena Walker, recognized that "if white women are benefited" by gaining the ballot, "so will colored women," because "both are helped and what uplifts one will surely assist the other." Virginians who subscribed to *The Crisis*, the journal of the National Association for the Advancement of Colored People (NAACP), could have read numerous essays and speeches that advocated woman suffrage, including two symposia on votes for African American women in September 1912 and August 1915. Women discussed suffrage at annual meetings of the Virginia State Federation of Colored Women's Clubs, but unfortunately, few records of discussions among Virginia women survive. Of the principal African American newspapers in the state (*Richmond Planet*, *St. Luke Herald*, *Newport News Star* and Norfolk's *Journal and Guide*), the *Planet* did not often report on the campaign for woman suffrage, and most or all copies of the other papers printed during the 1910s no longer exist. Moreover, records of African American women's organizations in Virginia are scattered and sadly incomplete for the period.[36]

At the July 1912 annual convention of the National Association of Colored Women, in Hampton, members from Hampton and Norfolk staged a suffrage parade as part of a pageant honoring prominent women. Seventy-two delegates from Virginia listened to, and perhaps some of them participated in, a discussion of the subject. Adella Hunt Logan, chair of the resolutions committee, "made an excellent plea for an enlarged intelligence on the subject of woman suffrage through systematic study of civic problems." The convention then "declared in favor of full woman suffrage and advocated the formation of political study clubs" for men and women.[37]

The following April, the executive committee of the National Association of Colored Women met in Arlington and Washington, D.C. President Margaret Washington, wife of the president of Tuskegee Institute, went out of her way to separate herself and other African American women who favored woman suffrage from the well-publicized acts of radical English suffragists. Many influential American white men condemned woman suffrage and all suffragists because of the English radicals' actions. "Our attitude toward the suffrage is of the conservative kind," Washington began. "We have not blown any houses with dynamite, nor have we been engaged in parading the streets in men's attire." She was careful not to alarm any white people who read about her speech later. Washington continued, "But of one thing I am certain, we are reading and studying the great questions which are to make for the good of the country, and when the vote is given to women as it surely will be where it is not already done, we shall be ready to cast our votes intelligently." Washington promised, clearly referring to exaggerated legends then current that some male African American voters had been easily corrupted during the nineteenth century, that women's votes would not be for sale for "a drink of liquor" or "two dollars."[38]

An editorial in a May 1913 issue of the *St. Luke Herald* emphatically stated the nature of the problem for African American women who wanted the vote. "The South is still under the blight and everlasting curse of slavery. The South is still gathering the vengeance of a just God. The South is still the land of bondage. There is no freedom in the South for either white or black. Race hate rules and predominates. There is no law for the Negro, but injustice and oppression—civilly, politically and educationally." The following year, the *St. Luke Herald* returned to the subject. "The women of the world are demanding and receiving the ballot; they are battling for it in every civilized country.…In the South white women want to join their sisters, but they are afraid lest in striving for the ballot for themselves they should in some way help the Negro woman."[39]

African Americans recognized that southern legislators and congressmen were unlikely to enfranchise women if it meant that black women could also wield a ballot. Not long after a suffrage parade in May 1914, the *St. Luke Herald*'s editor acknowledged that white women "even in Virginia, even in Richmond," were organizing and that southern politicians would help them "were they not afraid that suffrage for women, would include Negro women." The editor of the *Newport News Star* complained in 1918 that southern politicians knew "that it is impossible to expect to get rid of the black woman and, in consequence, they would use every means at their command to stop the passage of any measure which would show equal rights, equal justice and equal opportunity to the Negro woman."[40]

Some African American women who seized the opportunity to register and vote when it finally came in Virginia in 1920 were active members and officers of the Virginia State Federation of Colored Women's Clubs during the 1910s. Chief among them was Janie Porter Barrett of Hampton. She was the daughter of a seamstress and was born in Georgia only a few weeks after the end of slavery there. She was more fortunate than the large majority of her generation and attended and graduated from Hampton Normal and Agricultural Institute (later Hampton University) in Virginia. After a short career teaching, Barrett plunged into social service work and founded the Locust Street Social Settlement in Hampton, a counterpart for poor African Americans of the more famous Hull House settlement that Jane Addams and

Ellen Starr had founded for immigrants in Chicago. Barrett was a founder of the Virginia State Federation of Colored Women's Clubs in 1908 and served as its president until 1932. The federation founded and for many years she conducted the Industrial Home School for Colored Girls (later the Virginia Industrial School for Colored Girls and after 1950 the Janie Porter Barrett School for Girls) in Hanover County. Throughout her career, Barrett promoted education and social services for African Americans and often worked closely and productively with white women who shared the same devotion to children and education.[41]

JANIE PORTER BARRETT

Janie Porter Barrett, longtime president of the Virginia State Federation of Colored Women's Clubs. *Library of Virginia.*

It is a curious coincidence of early twentieth-century Virginia history that two of the best-known and most influential social reformers—one white, one black—were both named Barrett, although there is no evidence that the husbands of Kate Waller Barrett and Janie Porter Barrett were related to each other. The work of the two Barretts on behalf of women and children was very similar in several respects, and their parallel careers also coincided chronologically. It is also curious that of all the well-known women in Virginia engaged in social reform at that time, they and Lila Meade Valentine were among the few married women commonly known as and referred to by their given, maiden and surnames rather than by their husbands' names.

As in all the racially segregated southern states with parallel black and white social reform organizations, African American women in Virginia who supported votes for women did not seek to join the all-white Equal Suffrage League of Virginia, nor did they form a separate African American state organization. Keenly aware of the prejudice against African American voting that opponents of woman suffrage publicly announced and that some advocates also entertained, they perhaps declined to jeopardize the cause of all women by openly seeking the vote for themselves.

WORK LIKE HELL AND EDUCATE!

The campaign for woman suffrage was difficult enough, already, even without the complications racism caused, and required dedicated and time-consuming work. Members of the Equal Suffrage League distributed thousands of pieces of suffrage literature to influence people interested in women's rights, children, public health, education and political corruption. The league sponsored hundreds of events throughout the state. It conducted contests for the best student essays in support of woman suffrage, and it sometimes staged suffrage plays. Local leagues participated in community parades, decorating vehicles with signs and banners. Suffragists staffed booths at state and county fairs, speaking at those fairs and at church socials, in front of courthouses on court day, at schools, in movie theaters and often on street corners, wherever they could find or assemble an audience.

The league's executive secretary, Alice Overbey Taylor, reported from Richmond early in May 1915 that "our Mayor refused to permit the suffragists to do street speaking. In the absence of an ordinance stating that

Local leagues participated in parades, such as this one in Norfolk about 1915. *Sargeant Memorial Collection, Norfolk Public Library.*

The Equal Suffrage League of Virginia regularly staffed booths at state and county fairs, as at the Virginia State Fair in 1910. *The Valentine.*

this could be done. There was no ordinance to the contrary and the City Attorney said that there was no reason why we should not be allowed to speak. The Mayor, however, was obdurate and so we had to content ourselves with speaking from an automobile in the Capitol Square divided from the street only by an iron railing. This was a quiet corner, though, and in spite of fife and drum, I don't think we attracted more than a hundred people." At a rally there on May 1, 1915, however, Rabbi Edward Nathan Calisch, of Richmond's Congregation Beth Ahabah, made a major address to a large audience of men and women in support of votes for women.[42]

Suffragists in Norfolk faced no recorded impediments such as the mayor of Richmond imposed. The acting chief of police in Norfolk authorized the city's "Equal Suffrage League President Mrs. W.J. Adams"—Pauline Adams—"to speak on streets, on Monument Square, Feb. 10, 1913." Officials in some other cities were more sympathetic than the mayor of Richmond, but none, so far as extant documents show, went so far as Norfolk's Mayor Wyndham R. Mayo, who consented to be elected a vice president of the Norfolk league in 1915 and 1916.[43]

Suffragists staged a rally at the Virginia State Capitol on May 1, 1915, national Equal Suffrage Day. *The Valentine.*

CITY OF NORFOLK
Office CHIEF OF POLICE.

Feb. 10   1913

Permission is hereby granted to *Equal Suffrage League, President Mrs. W. J. adams to speak on streets, on Monument Square, Feb 10, 1913*

on condition that the holder will not obstruct the streets in any way, but so conduct said business as to prevent complaints being lodged at Headquarters. This permit may be revoked with or without cause.

W. P. Foch Capt 1st Pre
Acting CHIEF OF POLICE

Norfolk police issued a permit for Pauline Adams to speak about suffrage in downtown Norfolk in 1913. *Library of Virginia.*

Equal Suffrage League officers arriving in Capitol Square. *VCU Libraries*.

On the back of a photograph of league officials in an automobile at one of the capitol rallies in Richmond, somebody recorded the names of the suffragists but not the name of their African American driver. One wonders what he thought as he drove the prosperous white ladies on their rounds during the campaign for votes for women scarcely more than a decade after the Constitutional Convention of 1901–2 had deprived almost all African American men of the right to vote. Similarly, when one of the cars representing the Norfolk league in the city's 1915 Labor Day parade carried "a mother with two children and their colored nurse, with the placard in front, 'Women want the vote to protect their homes and children,'" did the African American woman riding in the car presumably to keep an eye on the children quietly support woman suffrage herself?[44]

In the 1917 annual report from the league branch at the University of Virginia, Marjorie J. Paul added a postscript couplet that epitomized the spirit of the suffragists, "Get up early, go to bed late / Work like Hell and educate!" For the most active suffragists, the couplet aptly described their devotion to the cause. Lila Meade Valentine made an average of two speeches a week during 1913 and once spoke in Hampton "at a Public

Meeting with People hooting outside." On another speaking occasion, somebody threw pepper in her face. Adèle Clark often set up her easel on a Richmond sidewalk and began to paint, which attracted curious people to whom she then delivered a lecture on votes for women. Clark spoke on street corners so often that she later quipped, "It reached the point where I couldn't see a fireplug without beginning 'Ladies and gentlemen.'"[45]

4

EVERLASTINGLY AT IT

ORGANIZING VIRGINIA SUFFRAGISTS

The year 1911, the second full year of the Equal Suffrage League of Virginia, concluded with the second annual state convention in Richmond. The members reelected Lila Meade Valentine president and elected or reelected Pauline Adams of Norfolk, Nannie C. Davis of Williamsburg, Elizabeth Lewis of Lynchburg and Sophie Meredith of Richmond as vice presidents; Ellen Tompkins Kidd as treasurer; and Alice M. Tyler, also of Richmond, as corresponding secretary.

The year 1912 opened with the regular session of the Virginia General Assembly. The league submitted petitions that endorsed woman suffrage from several cities, including one from Richmond, where women organized in the city's several wards to canvass for signatures. Several league members, including Mary Johnston, addressed the Senate's Committee on Privileges and Elections, which unanimously voted not to recommend a suffrage amendment to the state constitution. Hill Montague, a member of the General Assembly from Richmond, introduced an amendment in the House of Delegates. Valentine, Johnston, Lewis, Agnes Dillon Randolph, Edmonia Barksdale and popular Richmond novelist Kate Langley Bosher all spoke on its behalf before the House Committee on Privileges and Elections. However, the full House defeated the motion 85 to 12.[1]

Tyler reflected in her secretary's report of March 2, 1912, that "the recent campaign in the Virginia legislature has made evident to the Equal Suffrage League of Va. its strength." She meant skillful leaders who were intelligent, dedicated and excellent speakers and who had personal and family connections to many influential political leaders. On the other hand, she continued, "it has also made evident its weakness—that of lack of organization. The work that must occupy the Virginia suffragists during the time between now and the year 1914" when the General Assembly next met "must be the work of active organization."[2]

Carrie Chapman Catt, then president of National American Woman Suffrage Association, urged state suffrage groups to organize like political parties with local chapters and regional, or congressional district, coordinators. Valentine, who had spent the summer of 1911 in England where she observed the work of English suffragists, agreed. During 1912 and 1913 the league created a statewide organization that resembled the organizational structures

Carrie Chapman Catt, president of the National American Woman Suffrage Association. *Library of Congress.*

that Democrats and Republicans had in Virginia. The state league formed city, county and town leagues and appointed ten congressional district committee chairs.

MAKING NEW CONVERTS

Equal Suffrage League officers immediately began what became a five-year organizational campaign. Tyler sent letters to women all over the state early in March 1912. "The Equal Suffrage League of Virginia, of which I am the Corresponding Secretary," her standard letter began, "is most anxious to form an auxiliary league in your community and I am writing to you, and a number of your neighbors, hoping to enlist your interest and support along with theirs, in arranging for a public meeting, at which Mrs. B.B. Valentine, president of our state body, and Miss Mary Johnston, author of 'The Long Roll', can talk to an audience in your midst and awaken an active realization and civic and state responsibility among so important a group of Virginia women." As women in the state headquarters almost always did, she enclosed some suffrage literature to assist in building local support.[3]

Top: Letterhead of the Equal Suffrage League of Virginia in 1915. *Library of Virginia*.

Bottom: Georgiette Clarke Holmes of Surry County joined the Equal Suffrage League in 1915. *Library of Virginia*.

Valentine and Johnston, in their first such foray since their trips to Norfolk and Roanoke in 1910 and 1911, traveled together to Fredericksburg at the end of the first week in March 1912. Johnston's friend Janetta FitzHugh put them up in her house and arranged for a venue at which they could speak. A few days later, on March 12, eight women organized the Equal Suffrage League of Fredericksburg and elected FitzHugh president. She remained president until 1920.

Valentine and Johnston continued north to Alexandria, where Kate Waller Barrett arranged for them to speak on March 8 and 9. They organized the Equal Suffrage League of Alexandria on March 12. The members of the new league elected Barrett president, even though they knew that as an internationally known advocate for women she would be away from the city frequently. (An Equal Suffrage League record from 1916 identified her as "President-at-Large" with writer and Virginia historian Rose Mortimer Ellzey MacDonald as "acting president.")[4]

Less than two months later, on May 4, 1912, Johnston spoke in Staunton and organized a league with fifteen members. Twenty-seven women founded the Equal Suffrage League of Newport News on April 13, 1912, and nine women formed the Equal Suffrage League of Harrisonburg (later renamed the Equal Suffrage League of Rockingham County) on July 13. On August 22, twenty-eight women formed the Equal Suffrage League of Culpeper County, and after Valentine spoke in the western mountain town of Covington, sixty people formed a league there on September 18. Valentine and Ellie Putney formed the Equal Suffrage League of Wytheville in the new Wythe County Courthouse on October 5. The thirty-five founding members elected Putney president.

Valentine and Johnston joined forces on a brief tour through southwestern Virginia early in October. On October 8, they both spoke in Marion, and forty-three women formed a league there. Valentine was pleased at the "very large and representative audience." She reported to the Richmond office, "Mary was introduced by Judge Fudge an old Confederate veteran and I by Hon. A.T. Lincoln. Rev. Mr. Harris, Baptist minister, opened with prayer. All three men were converts….Went last night to a large reception, where we received much attention and made new converts." Valentine and Johnston went on a few miles farther south to speak in Bristol, where on October 11, forty-four women founded a league in that border city. A 1915 note on the Bristol league recorded that three of its members belonged to the Woman's Chamber of Commerce, Bristol, one of the earliest known references to a local businesswomen's group of the kind in the state.[5]

The women who joined Equal Suffrage Leagues in southwestern Virginia during the initial organizing demonstrated that the cause of woman suffrage was not confined to any one portion of the state or to large cities. In fact, Johnston and Valentine received several invitations to speak in the southwest before they made their organizing trip in the fall of 1912. Twenty-five women, apparently acting on their own, formed the Equal Suffrage League of Pulaski County on November 22, 1912. As in some other communities, initial enthusiasm there did not sustain itself. "The Pulaski women are very lukewarm concerning this movement," a woman who briefly resided in the county complained to Valentine early in 1915. "I have only been here a few months but understand they have tried a 'League' here with little success, altho many joined it." Several women founded a separate league in the town of Pulaski in October 1916, but it may not have been very active, either.[6]

Valentine explained to Elizabeth Lewis how league officers selected dates and places for speaking engagements. "Today," she wrote on June 23, 1915, "we have a letter from Mrs. Calvert of Sperryville saying that our best chance for Rappahannock County was to speak at Washington the County seat, on Court day from the steps of the Court House. This will be on the second Monday, July 12th.…I find it the great opportunity for getting at the voters. You see, you get a ready made audience." Court day—the day each month that the county court met—had been a social and political occasion of importance in Virginia for nearly three hundred years and almost always furnished "a ready made audience." On July 12, Lewis and Roberta Wellford, an Equal Suffrage League founder, spoke at the Rappahannock County courthouse and organized a new ten-member league.[7]

Suffragists spoke on court day as often as possible. In 1916, league secretary Ida Mae Thompson began a request to the circuit court judge who held a monthly court in the town of Bedford by writing, "Many of the Judges throughout the State have kindly given permission for Mrs. Valentine, President of the Equal Suffrage League of Virginia, and other of our speakers, to speak from the Court House steps, or in case of bad weather in the Court House, on Court day. We are writing now to ask if you will also grant such permission to Mrs. Dexter Otey, Treasurer of the Lynchburg Equal Suffrage League, to speak on Equal Suffrage, on July 1st, at Bedford City," court day at the county seat. "Mrs. Otey is a highly cultured woman and a most attractive speaker," Thompson concluded, "and we feel sure that all who hear her will be more than pleased."[8]

In that instance, their usually reliable plan failed, in part because of confusion about court day in the county. Thompson evidently failed to consult Eugénie Macon Yancey, president of the Equal Suffrage League of Bedford County since Valentine founded it on May 18, 1913. A brief, undated biographical note preserved in the papers of the Equal Suffrage League of Virginia described Yancey as then "the most important woman in her town, socially and civically. She is a leader in all social functions and it is said that any thing meant for civic improvement is sure of success if it meets with her approval." Had Yancey had an opportunity to comment, she might have saved Otey an embarrassment.[9]

Elizabeth Otey (*left*) and her mother, Elizabeth Lewis, of Lynchburg, about 1915. *Jones Memorial Library, Lynchburg.*

In response to Thompson's request, the judge ordered the janitor to allow Otey into the courthouse on July 1, but that was a Saturday, and the judge had rescheduled the meeting of the court to Monday, July 3. Otey rearranged her travel plans and arrived on the appointed day to find that the grand jury was in session and nobody else was present. She learned later in the day that the "country people" crowded into town not on court day in that county, as was customary elsewhere, but on the fourth Monday in the month when the county board of supervisors met. "That used to be the Court day," a local woman informed Otey, before it was changed more than a decade earlier. The "country people were accustomed to assemble then," she learned, "and still continue to do so." Otey nevertheless spoke in the afternoon to a small gathering "from a motor," standing in an open-top automobile.[10]

Elizabeth Dabney Langhorne Lewis Otey (Mrs. Dexter Otey in the parlance of the time) was indeed a "highly cultured" and remarkable woman. She was the daughter of league vice president Elizabeth Lewis and a first cousin of Lady Astor. She had attended Randolph-Macon Woman's College (later Randolph College), graduated from Bryn Mawr, where she participated in the musical life of the college, and studied at the University of Chicago before she earned a doctorate in economics from the University of Berlin in 1907 with a dissertation on the cotton industry in the southern states. She worked for more than two years for the Department of Labor in Washington, which in 1910 published *The Beginnings of Child Labor Legislation in Certain States: A Comparative Study*, which she and two other researchers prepared. After she married a Lynchburg businessman in 1910, Otey returned to her hometown; had a daughter; completed work on a monograph, *Employers' Welfare Work*, which the Bureau of Labor Statistics published in 1913; and joined her mother in the campaign for woman suffrage.[11]

ACTIVE ORGANIZATION

At the annual Equal Suffrage League state convention in Norfolk on October 24 and 25, 1912, about forty delegates posed for a joint photograph, and it appeared on the front page of the *Virginian-Pilot and Norfolk Landmark*. Total league membership then stood at about 1,500. The work of organizing new leagues increased apace. Suffragists formed about a dozen local leagues in 1912, and they created more than two dozen in

1913. Valentine reported to the state convention on October 14, 1913, that the Farmville league she helped organize three days earlier was the state's thirty-ninth. League officers organized at least ten more leagues in 1914. Between the beginning of 1915 and the country's entrance into World War I in the spring of 1917, Valentine, Lewis and other league leaders organized more than seventy-five new leagues.

During 1915, Lewis formed leagues in Front Royal, in the counties of Rappahannock, Nelson, Halifax, Buckingham, Amherst and Amelia and two in Campbell County; she and Otey jointly spoke in the western mountain towns of Clifton Forge and Covington in May of that year. Faith W. Morgan, president of the Newport News league, also spoke and helped organize leagues in her vicinity, on the Eastern Shore and south of the James River.

Valentine was extraordinarily active. She had no children to care for, and her husband's income allowed her to be free of time-consuming household responsibilities, but her health was often an obstacle. She suffered from painful and prolonged migraine headaches, was susceptible to respiratory infections and had occasional attacks of severe gastrointestinal problems that disabled her for weeks at a time. Nevertheless, in at least seventeen separate trips from her home and headquarters in Richmond in 1915, Valentine organized twenty-one or more leagues on the Eastern Shore, in southeastern Virginia, in the southern Piedmont and in northern Virginia. Moreover, she and her husband also spent two weeks early in September at Atlantic City where under doctor's orders he recuperated from an attack of bronchitis. He rested, but she did not. She made suffrage speeches at the corner of Atlantic and North Carolina Avenues in Atlantic City and took the hour-long trolley ride down to Ocean City, New Jersey, to speak there. In addition to speaking in New Jersey and Virginia, Valentine also accepted invitations to campaign for woman suffrage and spoke in West Virginia, Tennessee, Pennsylvania and both North and South Carolina.

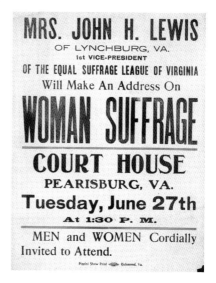

MRS. JOHN H. LEWIS
OF LYNCHBURG, VA.
1st VICE-PRESIDENT
OF THE EQUAL SUFFRAGE LEAGUE OF VIRGINIA
Will Make An Address On

WOMAN SUFFRAGE

COURT HOUSE
PEARISBURG, VA.
Tuesday, June 27th
At 1:30 P. M.
MEN and WOMEN Cordially Invited to Attend.

The leaders of the Equal Suffrage League spoke throughout the commonwealth. *Library of Virginia.*

Almost all suffrage activists volunteered their time, and the state officers may have paid their own travel expenses. Relying on volunteers posed challenges to organizing and directing the work of local leagues as well as managing the state headquarters. Kate Waller Barrett, Adèle Clark, Ellen Tompkins Kidd, Roberta Wellford and others gave suffrage talks when they could or helped found local leagues, but most of them also had continuing professional or family responsibilities that meant they could not be as active or on the road as much as Valentine and Lewis. Valentine's unmarried sisters, Marianne Everard Meade and Kate Fontaine Meade, were among the founding members of the Equal Suffrage League, but league records contain only a few references to their work. Newspaper reports documented their attendance at league conventions, but most of their work was behind the scenes. Their names and more than two dozen others appear on an early 1917 report of volunteers in the state headquarters "who have helped in folding the enormous quantity of literature distributed." Other suffragists elsewhere almost certainly contributed to the campaign in ways that produced little or no documentary evidence.[12]

On a list of Culpeper County suffragists Valentine sent to Lewis in the summer of 1915, she noted that the husband of the league president had died the previous year, and since then she "has not written to us." The league in Petersburg had what Valentine described in the spring of 1916 as "a good membership" with about seventy-five supporters, but "the leader, an active young woman, married and went to North Carolina to live." Since then, Valentine lamented, "I have tried in vain to secure another leader, but they have co-operated with us in speaking at the County Fair, last October and securing a good petition to be presented to our Legislature." Ellie Putney, founding president of the Equal Suffrage League of Wytheville, actively participated in league work and in organizing and speaking through 1916, but she fell ill and moved to her daughter's home in Baltimore, where she died in 1918.[13]

Corresponding secretary Alice M. Tyler died in May 1913, but equally committed and able Alice O. Taylor took her place. Taylor had a lively wit and published both prose and verse in local newspapers. She wrote strongly worded letters to editors of Richmond newspapers to criticize people who opposed allowing women to vote and to expose fallacies in their reasoning. In July 1913, she attacked S. Gordon Cumming, a former legislator and potential candidate for attorney general, who had stated that he did not wish to see women given the vote, which would degrade them from "the high pedestal on which God placed" them. Taylor took sharp aim with her pen or typewriter and shot back, "I had taken Mr. Cumming to be an honorable gentleman," she began, "but since he claims to be on a plane lower than woman I, as a woman, protest against his aspiring to the position of Attorney-General of Virginia, and deny his fitness to govern those who, according to his asseveration, are above him." For one reason or another, Cumming did not run for attorney general that year.[14]

From 1913 to 1915, Taylor was executive secretary and one of the office managers of the Equal Suffrage League headquarters. She was a prominent participant in the state league's work and conventions and held the comparable office in the Richmond city league. The May 1915 issue of the *American Home Journal* included her short story "Within the Ring" in support of woman suffrage. With her own resources, Taylor financed publication of the eight-page monthly *Virginia Suffrage News*, which became the official organ of the Equal Suffrage League. With Taylor as publisher and managing editor and Mary Ellen Pollard Clarke as editor-in-chief, they published the first issue in October 1914. It included the text of a speech supporting woman suffrage by Secretary of State William Jennings Bryan, a suffrage essay by Mary Johnston, both prose and verse by Clarke, news from local chapters of the Equal Suffrage League and reports on activities of suffragists in other states. And over the initials A.O.T., Taylor ridiculed several opponents of woman suffrage, including one unidentified member of the General Assembly.

Clarke worked closely with Taylor in the Equal Suffrage League office. Long active with Valentine in the Richmond Education Association, she was also a founder of one of Richmond's elite literary societies, the Every Monday Club and, later, in 1922, became the first woman to serve on the State Library Board. Clarke was chair of the league's Third District Committee in 1915 and about that time published *Human-Rights Not in Violation of States' Rights: An Appeal to the Men of Virginia*, which argued that granting women the vote would not undermine the recent disfranchisement of African American men. She also composed the text for the leaflet "Equal Suffrage and the Negro Vote" that suffragists circulated to combat opponents' charges that woman suffrage would endanger white supremacy. Clarke no doubt relied on legal advice on that subject from her brother, state attorney general John Garland Pollard, who also supported woman suffrage.[15]

In the winter of 1914–15, Taylor suffered an illness not described in surviving league correspondence. Valentine lamented that Taylor's "illness, and also the failure of her income from some cotton interest in the South"

VIRGINIA SUFFRAGE NEWS

Vol. 1, No. 2   RICHMOND, VA. NOVEMBER 1914   Subscription $1.00

"THREE HILLS," THE HOME OF MARY JOHNSTON

"Let me live in my home by the side of the road
And be a friend to man."

The day of secluded goodness and cloistered learning is past. These have gone the way of all things which the time-spirit has made ineffectual. They served God's plan in the world, and are now reverenced only as part of the glorious past.

To-day, men and women are looking out from their own private abodes, where "the race of men go by," and are eager to help on "the highway of life." In this day of social awakening, even our homes are being socialized in the spirit of co-operation and fellowship.

Such a home is that of Mary Johnston, the distinguished authoress and suffragist. It stands amidst the beautiful mountains of Bath County, Virginia, near the Warm Springs. Here she might hide herself from "the madding crowd," and just send a message once a year through her books to the outside world. But her heart is too big for this—it beats in sympathy with every human interest and every human aspiration. She gives herself and also her home generously to her community, and gladly do they respond to her hospitality.

Every Saturday evening, the halls and chambers and grounds of this beautiful home are thrown wide open, and Miss Johnston, with her sisters, welcomes the young and the old of Bath County. They come from far and near to have a happy time in discussing events of current and past history, and afterwards games and refreshments have their place in the program. The distinguished hostess is a part of it all, entering with zest into the pleasures as well as the polemics of the evening.

Miss Elizabeth Johnston is President of this Neighborhood Association, and is responsible for its program of instruction and entertainment. Miss Eloise Johnston has her share also in contributing to the happy times of these wonderful evenings at "Three Hills."   M. P. C.

ON TO ROANOKE.   ON TO NASHVILLE

Virginia Suffrage News for November 1914. *Library of Virginia.*

with which she had helped fund *Virginia Suffrage News*, "made it necessary to suspend publication for a few months." *Virginia Suffrage News* ceased publication after a mere three monthly issues and never resumed. "Mrs. Taylor takes no salary now of course." In September 1915, Valentine informed Jessie Townsend, president of the Equal Suffrage League of Norfolk, "Our offices in Richmond are in much trouble." The mother of one regular volunteer "was paralyzed last week and is very ill," and the daughter of another "lost her baby very suddenly." Valentine concluded, "You heard of Alice Taylor's loss. Her sister's death makes it necessary for

Equal Suffrage League office in Richmond about 1915. *VCU Libraries*.

her to be with her mother constantly hence we have lost her invaluable services for several months to come I fear."[16]

Edith Clark Cowles and Ida Mae Thompson took over running the state headquarters and were more than up to the job. Thompson became a secretary of the Equal Suffrage League in 1913 and worked at state headquarters until the league dissolved after its work was done in 1920. She threw herself into the work. Thompson filled pages of dime-store notebooks with her neat script, usually writing with a well-sharpened pencil. Thrifty, she used the backs of envelopes and outdated letterhead stationery to record information, make notes and copy addresses. Thompson typed letters, ordered supplies, scheduled speaking engagements and mailed broadsides and bulletins to local leagues. While Valentine and the others traveled, made speeches and organized suffragists, Thompson dealt with a variety of practical concerns and unpleasant tasks. She intervened with the landlord when he raised the rent for the state headquarters and tracked down a handyman when the roof leaked. Her task was an important one—to keep the Equal Suffrage League's state headquarters running smoothly.[17]

NEW LEADERS

The organizing work brought new leaders such as Clarke, Cowles and Thompson into action throughout the state. Faith Walcott Morgan, a native of New York City, was one. She and her banker husband moved to Virginia early in the decade to be near her sister who worked at Hampton Normal and Agricultural Institute. Morgan and her husband both supported votes for women prior to his death in his fishing boat, the *Suffragette*, in 1916. She joined the Equal Suffrage League, marched with other Virginia suffragists in the massive March 1913 parade in Washington, D.C., and late that year she and Ellen Llewellyn Robinson collected about 1,200 signatures in Hampton and Newport News on a petition to the General Assembly in support of woman suffrage. In 1915, Morgan was elected chair of the

Faith Walcott Morgan, president of the Equal Suffrage League of Newport News and a vice president of the Equal Suffrage League of Virginia. *Courtesy of the Morgan family.*

Equal Suffrage League of Newport News and assisted in the formation of other leagues in southeastern Virginia. She also returned to New York for several months in 1917 to assist in the campaign for woman suffrage there.[18]

Eager Missouri native Ellen Llewellyn Robinson lived near Morgan and joined the Equal Suffrage League about the same time as she. Robinson proselytized shipyard workers on their lunch breaks as part of the Newport News league's campaign to recruit white working-class men and women. Robinson was chair of the First Congressional District Committee and divided her time between working for suffrage there, organizing chapters elsewhere in Virginia and working at the National American Woman Suffrage Association office in Washington, D.C. She addressed an audience she estimated at fifteen thousand people at the annual reunion of Confederate veterans at Fisher's Hill, in Shenandoah County, on August 5, 1916, but none of the half-dozen or more newspaper accounts of

Eudora Ramsay was a field organizer for the National American Woman Suffrage Association from 1915 to 1917. *Library of Virginia.*

the reunion mentioned Robinson's speech. She was extremely industrious, insomuch that Morgan interjected into her 1915 annual report an aside that "Miss Ellen L. Robinson, of Newport News and Washington, is <u>not</u> a whole League by herself."[19]

Late in 1915, Lila Meade Valentine engaged Eudora Woolfolk Ramsay, an organizer for the National American Woman Suffrage Association, to work two months in Virginia for seventy-five dollars plus expenses. A college graduate, former teacher and daughter of a pastor of one of Richmond's Baptist churches, Ramsay was well educated, well experienced and well qualified. Before, as well as between, her several sojourns in Virginia, Ramsay spoke on behalf of woman suffrage and did organizational work in West Virginia, Tennessee, South Carolina, Pennsylvania, Oklahoma, New York and Maine. Valentine described her as young, attractive and a "fine speaker" who had "spent four months as paid organizer in ten counties of Pennsylvania, all ten of her counties went for suffrage!" Ramsay "goes to a perfectly new place," Valentine continued, "calls on the minister, gets the names of prominent women and before long has the meeting arranged. She spoke three or four times a day and almost every Sunday night in a church."[20]

In December 1915, a newspaper confirmed Valentine's evaluation. "At King William Courthouse," the *Richmond Times-Dispatch* reported, Ramsay "was allowed to speak in the courtroom by the courtesy of Judge Claggett B. Jones. About twenty men remained" after the court adjourned, "but in a few minutes after she began to speak, the courthouse could not hold all who wanted to hear. A great many men signed the petition to be presented to the Legislature. After motoring forty miles and speaking at the courthouse," Ramsay traveled to West Point and "spoke in Owen's Hall in the evening to a large audience of both men and women. After speaking forty-one minutes she accepted an invitation from the proprietor of a local theater to speak between reels at a moving picture show."[21]

After Ramsay's first brief speaking tour in Virginia, she went to Tennessee and South Carolina, but she returned to work in Virginia late in 1916.

She organized Colonial Place chapter in Norfolk County on December 5, and Valentine arranged for her to speak at the courthouse in Heathsville, Northumberland County, where on December 13 she organized a new league. Ramsay made favorable impressions during her several short tenures working in Virginia. During her sojourns in Virginia, she established seventeen leagues, reorganized seven and opened six new suffrage centers.

Ramsay worked in Oklahoma before she returned to Virginia again just as the nation entered World War I. Lists of contributions she collected in April 1917 and her expense account for May, both in the Equal Suffrage League of Virginia Records, and her reports to headquarters, now in the Adèle Clark Papers, document her almost relentless schedule for six weeks in the spring of 1917. Those records contain the most detailed account of how Virginia suffragists organized local suffrage leagues.

In April, Ramsay spent about ten days working her way south through the counties of Accomack and Northampton on Virginia's Eastern Shore, where she delivered ten suffrage lectures in ten towns and organized six new leagues. She began the month of May more than one hundred miles west of the Eastern Shore. Ramsay spoke at three meetings on the first two days of the month in Nottoway County, one in a theater with 150 people, another with 75 people and a third with 25. Ramsay spent May 3, 5 and 6 in Richmond at the state headquarters. During the night of May 3–4, she traveled by train northwest to Scottsville to reorganize the league there and returned on the night train to Richmond for the next two days. Ramsay then rode the night train to Portsmouth, where on

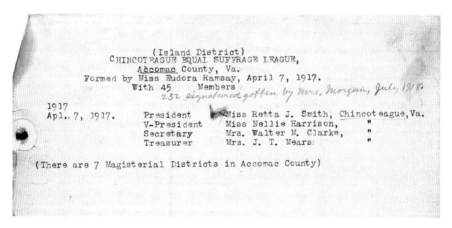

Ramsay formed a chapter of the Equal Suffrage League in Chincoteague on Virginia's Eastern Shore in 1917. *Library of Virginia.*

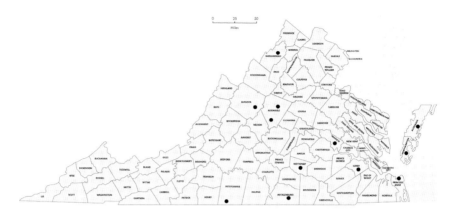

Places where Eudora Ramsay spoke in April–May 1917. *Library of Virginia.*

May 7, she spoke and conducted a meeting and then returned on the night train to Richmond.

Ramsay made eight trips from Richmond during the month, one of them extending for ten days and nights. She traveled to South Hill and Danville, on the North Carolina border; to Surry County between Richmond and Portsmouth; to Ivy, west of Charlottesville; and to the Shenandoah Valley towns of Waynesboro and Woodstock. Ramsay spoke to more than 1,200 people (almost certainly all of them white) in at least twenty-seven venues, traveling more than one thousand miles. She spent $81.20 on food, lodging, transportation and incidental expenses in May. The expense accounts do not specifically indicate how much of her travel was by bus, train or automobile (at one point during her work she owned a car and drove herself), but during May she tipped Pullman car porters eight times, which indicates that she rode in sleeping cars for parts or all of eight nights.

Ramsay's April and May 1917 work concluded the league's campaign to organize suffragists in the state's towns, cities, and counties. During the war, the leagues in cities shifted their attentions, as officers of the National American Woman Suffrage Association recommended, to support war-related activities, such as promoting purchase of war bonds.

At least three colleges had Equal Suffrage Leagues. Randolph-Macon Woman's College (later Randolph College) in Lynchburg had a league that Elizabeth Otey helped found in 1913. It consistently had between 125 and 150 members each year. Westhampton College, a women's college affiliated with the University of Richmond, also had a chapter formed in January 1918. Of the several leagues in Albemarle County, the largest with 325 members in 1916 was the University Chapter, founded on an unrecorded date before July 30, 1913, with two male University of Virginia faculty members as vice presidents.

The records of the Equal Suffrage League and league correspondence in the Adèle Clark Papers preserve a large amount of information about the founding of most of the 145 known local leagues. Residents of almost every city and county in the state formed leagues during the decade. It is possible that some of the other towns and counties for which records do not exist may have also had leagues. For most of the leagues, few or no records survive. As Janetta FitzHugh reported from Fredericksburg in the mid-1930s, she had kept documents "relating to early work in the State and to the local work done here for years, but finally, being pressed for room to retain such matter, destroyed them all." Something similar almost certainly took place elsewhere.[22]

Founding dates and names of founding officers for more than one hundred county, city and town leagues are preserved in the Equal Suffrage League of Virginia Records. The basic document for most leagues is an undated typed list that league officials prepared in the state office. Several memoranda also include some membership numbers. Some minutes of meetings and annual reports survive for a few cities, and newspaper reports provide founding dates and other information for a few others. The records for no locality are complete, and for a few little more than the undated memoranda still exist. Very few of the local league records contain membership lists or records of the work they did. As was common at the time, most of the married or widowed women are identified only by their husband's names.

EVERLASTINGLY AT IT

Cities had the largest and most active leagues. Elizabeth Lewis's November 1914 annual report as president of the Lynchburg league gave details of the activities and programs the league sponsored there. The members held "monthly meetings thus far in private houses but this term, the Y.M.C.A. of Lynchburg—in the face of violent opposition by the local press—has given the use of its spacious Auditorium for a course of free lectures to be delivered under the auspices of the Club." Lewis reported optimistically, "Equal Suffrage sentiment is growing in Lynchburg, in spite of intense and sometimes devisive opposition on the part of the local democratic (?)

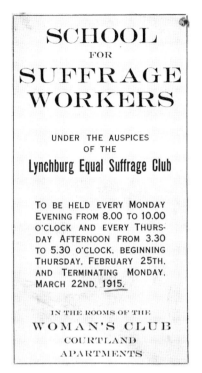

SCHOOL
FOR
SUFFRAGE
WORKERS

UNDER THE AUSPICES
OF THE
Lynchburg Equal Suffrage Club

To be held every Monday
Evening from 8.00 to 10.00
o'clock and every Thurs-
day Afternoon from 3.30
to 5.30 o'clock, beginning
Thursday, February 25th,
and Terminating Monday,
March 22nd, 1915.

IN THE ROOMS OF THE
WOMAN'S CLUB
COURTLAND
APARTMENTS

A 1915 Lynchburg pamphlet for classes on how to advocate woman suffrage. *Library of Virginia.*

press." Her insertion of a parenthetical question mark after the adjective *democratic* indicated that although both of the city's newspapers were partisan Democratic papers, they were not in favor of the democratic reform of granting women the right to vote. "The better element of women are slowly awakening to its claims," Lewis nevertheless continued, "and also the better element of men. This winter a Men's League for Equal Suffrage will be formed which will give impetus to the movement. The Club works on undaunted—secure in the final triumph of this measure of equal justice and of popular right." On April 20, 1917, the Lynchburg league published five thousand copies of *The Lynchburg Woman's Suffrage News* with Elizabeth Otey as editor. Members sold copies on the streets, but no known copies survive.[23]

Some leagues also inserted themselves into local discussions of other issues relating to women. Members of the Norfolk league were especially concerned early in the decade about young women who worked at a local theater. Corresponding secretary Jessie Fremont Easton Townsend submitted the Norfolk league's informative 1912 annual report. She was a native Kentuckian who after she graduated from high school married a businessman in Zanesville, Ohio. They had two daughters and a son before they moved to Norfolk early in the 1890s. Her husband sold adding machines, typewriters and automobiles before he founded the Elizabeth Park and Land Company. She served at various times as the company's secretary-treasurer, vice president and president. An early member of the Equal Suffrage League of Norfolk, she was elected treasurer in 1911 and president in 1913. Townsend marched with other Virginians in the March 3, 1913 suffrage parade in Washington, D.C., attended state conventions regularly during the decade and conventions of the National American Woman Suffrage Association in 1914 and 1916. A vice president of the state league beginning in 1916, Townsend became one of Lila Meade Valentine's most trusted allies and one of the state league's most important leaders. The surviving correspondence between Townsend and Valentine is almost as valuable as Valentine's with Lewis for the insights it provides into the workings of the state league, the organization of local leagues and the development of policy and strategy.[24]

"Probably you would like to know how we raised money," Townsend began one section of her 1912 report from Norfolk. "Well I believe we went about it in a truly feminine way, the way women have raised things since time immemorial, a little here and a little there, everlastingly at it. A member who had a vacu[u]m cleaner rented it to other members so much a day, the proceeds going into the treasury of the league. Another whose cook made fine loaf bread and pies, had a standing weekly order from another member," probably an instance in which the paid work of an African American woman in the kitchen of a white woman aided the campaign of white women for the vote. A member "who found she had put up an over supply of catsup, peaches, jelly and so forth"—perhaps also with the assistance of a cook or other servant—"sold the surplus for the treasury." Another member "used her typewriter and spare hours.…We passed the hat at most of our evening gatherings. We went down into our own pockets as often as necessary and last but not least kept our expenses down to the minimum."[25]

The November 1914 annual report from the Equal Suffrage League of Norfolk was also detailed. Valentine had "appeared twice before the League, and was invited to address the monthly meeting of city teachers. A luncheon tendered Mrs. Valentine at the Y.W.C.A. was a pleasant incident of her visit, and gave members a chance to meet her.…During the year the League has resorted to several devices to raise money. 'The Suffragette' cracker has been sold on commission, two subscription card parties held, and a play entitled 'How the Vote was Won', given. This play was given at the Maury High School. A debate on Suffrage between High School societies filled out the rest of the program. The lack of funds seriously hampers the work of the league. Funds would mean permanent headquarters, and that would mean rapid growth." Nevertheless, "Suffrage sentiment grows slowly in Norfolk, the most hopeful evidence of growth in this section is the formation of the Portsmouth League and the Princess Ann[e] League. The Equal Suffrage League of Norfolk now has 443 members. Some old members were transferred to the Portsmouth and Princess Anne Leagues, so the growth is more than numbers show." Princess Anne County was

Left: Jessie Townsend was president of the Equal Suffrage League of Norfolk from 1913 to 1914. *VCU Libraries*.

Right: Jessie Townsend and other members of the ESL attended conventions of the National American Woman Suffrage Association. *Library of Virginia*.

adjacent to the city of Norfolk in the southeastern corner of the state; the city of Virginia Beach absorbed it in 1963.[26]

An undated manuscript titled "The Community Spirit at Lynnhaven" in the National American Woman Suffrage Association Papers preserves a long account of the work of women in the Lynnhaven neighborhood of Princess Anne County. References in the report to rising prices suggest that it may have been submitted during World War I. The author reported that the women held a banquet to raise money to erect a community house and also organized to build a library. "Women whose mother hearts are not content with mothering the two or more at their comfortable firesides," the writer explained, "women whose good housekeeping does not rest within their own acre lots, but whose mothering and good housekeeping is capable of reaching out to whatever will lead to the moral and intellectual uplift of all.…Real Community Spirit! It was not dead in old Princess Anne, only

The Equal Suffrage League of Richmond sold tickets to promote the suffrage film *Your Girl and Mine* playing at a local theater early in March 1915. *VCU Libraries*.

Antis : Indifferents : Suffragists

ALL INVITED TO HEAR

MRS. B. B. VALENTINE

President *of the* Equal Suffrage League *of* Virginia

SPEAK ON

EQUAL SUFFRAGE

In Hampton, April 21, at 8 P. M., at Y. M. C. A.

In Newport News, April 22, at 8 P. M.
In *the* Corporation Court Room, City Hall

ADMISSION FREE. COME—Bring Your Friends and Ask Questions

Under the Auspices of the Newport News Equal Suffrage League

The Equal Suffrage League of Virginia advertised appearances by its president Lila Meade Valentine, as in this 1914 card. *Library of Virginia*.

sleeping for a time!" The final lines contain the most important information: "And would you suspect it awoke first in the heart of Suffragists? Don't tell I said so, for Equal Suffrage is not yet popular in Princess Anne. They think they don't believe in it, but they do, for it is the spirit of personal liberty for which their ancestry fought and bled. Personal liberty, served up in a new style. They'll soon quit shying at it." The long report is signed, "A Suffragist who was there."[27]

The community event in Princess Anne County was undoubtedly not unique. In August 1916, Lila Meade Valentine spoke at a "suffrage rally and picnic, one of the first ever held in Virginia…at Goochland Courthouse on August 19th, and was very largely attended. It was an all-day affair and men and women came from over the entire county." It is likely that similar events occurred elsewhere in Virginia.[28]

LARGER THAN ANY WOMAN'S ORGANIZATION IN THE STATE

Leagues in neighboring cities and counties sometimes worked together. Norfolk and adjacent Norfolk County had several leagues that sometimes cooperated and sometimes quarreled about how much dues each league owed to support the work of the state league and the national association. Jessie Townsend spent many hours trying to solve problems and promote cooperation. Faith Morgan reported late in 1915 that the Hampton and Newport News leagues cooperated "in all their work. The membership of the two Leagues is so interwoven that it is hard to tell where one ends and the other begins." In fact, Morgan submitted annual reports from both leagues in the autumn of 1917. The Hampton league then had 285 members and the Newport News league 444.[29]

The city of Roanoke, Roanoke County, and the neighboring town of Salem all had equal suffrage leagues, and the separate Equal Franchise League in the city had a larger membership than any of them, 1,100 members by July 1916. (The meager surviving records do not explain why the city had two separate leagues.) The Equal Franchise League of Roanoke created its own suffrage library and organized the city's four wards with a chair and two assistants in each. "We have no dues," President Nannie Burks reported in 1915, "but always pass the collection basket, even if only two or three are present. We ask subscriptions. We did very well with a series of cake sales on the Market Square. At Easter we sold eggs....We get money if possible, without stealing from the neighbors."[30]

Each of the four leagues had its own officers, but Annie Barna Whitner belonged to both the city and county leagues, which reflected the circumstances of her life and the nature of the larger community. She and her civil engineer and businessman husband lived in the city until they grew prosperous enough to purchase a large estate in the county, near Salem. Whitner was elected a vice president of the Equal Suffrage League of Roanoke in 1913, and on September 13 of that year, she was the founding president of the Equal Suffrage League of Roanoke County. In December, she and four other women attended a two-week woman suffrage workshop in Washington, D.C., where she studied parliamentary procedures, effective lobbying techniques and how to conduct fundraising and canvassing efforts. In a short article titled "Women and War" that Whitner wrote for the November 1914 issue of *Virginia Suffrage News*, three months after World War I began in Europe, she adduced the war among the reasons why suffragists should "re-consecrate ourselves to our great work." Whitner predicted, "If we women lift our voices loud enough and long enough in protest and appeal they will be heard around the world, and in time women will share with men the power which shapes the fate of nations. And then that 'hell upon earth'—war—will cease, and peace will reign."[31]

Whitner and Lucinda Lee Terry, of the Roanoke city league, reportedly persuaded Delegate Holman Willis of the city of Roanoke to support woman suffrage in 1914, but the county's delegate and the senators who represented the area during the 1910s refused to endorse woman suffrage. "The activities of Roanoke City and County suffragists have so overlapped and been so intertwined with war relief work," Whitner explained in her 1916–17 annual report as president of the county league shortly after being elected a vice president of the state league, that "we hardly know which from tother."[32]

Suffragists sometimes provided state headquarters with references to local men who approved of woman suffrage and also about women who were related to influential men and might be able to persuade them to support equal suffrage. A 1919 note on the office memorandum for the Fredericksburg league indicated that President Janetta FitzHugh's brother-in-law Richard Henry Lee Chichester, then a circuit court judge and later a justice on the Supreme Court of Appeals, supported woman suffrage "& helps when called on." League officers in Campbell County near Lynchburg identified "Senator Robt. A. Russell, Rustburg (Suffragist)." The wife of

Senator John R. Saunders, who won election as attorney general in 1917, was a member of the league in the Middlesex County town of Saluda. In Charlotte County, "Mr. B.H. White," superintendent of a local school, "has been a good suffragist for 25 years and speaks for suffrage." In Fluvanna County, "Mr. Pembroke Pettit (Com. Atty.)," or commonwealth's attorney, and "Rev. F.G. Lavender" were both sympathetic. Brunswick County even had a "Men's Committee" for a time in 1915.[33]

The reports also included information on women whose contacts could be valuable, such as the "County President W.C.T.U." in Martinsville. Some members of the Woman's Christian Temperance Union held offices in local chapters of the Equal Suffrage League, but lacking local membership lists for most Equal Suffrage League chapters, it is not possible to know for certain how many suffragists were members of both. Temperance and prohibition organizations in Virginia were both active during the campaign for woman suffrage, but annual reports of the league and the WCTU do not disclose whether the two organizations often cooperated in Virginia as they did in some other states. Collaboration would seem a natural one. Temperance advocates had for decades been attempting to persuade state legislatures to enact laws to deal with problems alcohol consumption created, and the national organization endorsed woman suffrage in 1881.[34]

It is not entirely clear how effective the majority of the local leagues were in mobilizing public opinion, how active their officers were in keeping members energized or even what many of them accomplished. Some local leagues successfully campaigned for support of the cause with local newspaper editors and political leaders, but some leagues may have become inactive for want of enough members to carry on the work or because the Equal Suffrage League recommended that women divert their energies to war-related work in 1917 and 1918.

Equal Suffrage League officers occasionally went into the field to reorganize local leagues. Adèle Clark went to Fredericksburg in 1919 to reorganize Janetta FitzHugh's league there. That league's membership had grown from 35 in November 1915 to 325 in May 1918, so the reason for Clark's trip is not clear. Perhaps the membership had grown so large that the leaders needed advice about how to run so numerous an association of volunteers. In other instances, the reasons were obvious. Women in rural areas often found it difficult to arrange convenient meetings, and some of those leagues were inactive much of the time. The president of the league in rural Middlesex County reported in 1916 that because the scattered members "live in the country, many miles apart, it seems hard to do much."

Officers also allowed some local leagues to atrophy, give little assistance to the statewide campaign or lose momentum during the world war. Late in 1919, Elizabeth Lewis reported that she spoke to "a mixed—and rather small—audience at the School Auditorium" in the small south-central town of Keysville. "The League there is lukewarm, and has disintegrated like so many others." Annie Shackelford Smithey recalled from Hanover County in 1936, "About the time I joined it had <u>almost</u> disbanded."[35]

Lalla Smoot's 1916 annual report from Caroline County recounted her difficult work there on behalf of votes for women. "Can you not try to interest the professional men here in Bowling Green," she pleaded with the state headquarters, "they, it seems to me, hold the key to the situation here. The women are dependent upon them for their opinions on large questions, and in town, it seems, the professional men are dependent upon the people for their incomes! It is considered anarchy for women in small places to think for themselves." Smoot explained that women in the town appeared to believe that they should always follow the men in their thinking, "except about children (a big question to be sure), housekeeping and pink teas" at which women discussed politics in the absence of men or raised money for charity. "But when these prominent men stand as stone walls in a small town, what can a few women do, they soon find themselves exhausted."[36]

The *Big Stone Gap Post* in the southwestern county of Wise reported on the town's thirty-member league in April 1916. The report revealed more enthusiasm than achievement. "That the Gap is not going to be left behind in any progressive movement," it began, "is proved again by the fact that an Equal Suffrage League has been in existence at this place for the past year, and while no active work has been done, no parades, and no speeches made on the capitol steps, yet the League believes just as firmly in Votes for Women as if all these things had been done by the maids and matrons of the Gap."[37]

A few months later, the bulletin of the Equal Suffrage League of Virginia reported that Cora Benedict, president of the league in Big Stone Gap, had "secured a vacant room above the Moving Picture Show" on Wood Avenue "to be used for a club room, rest room and library. At Mrs. Benedict's request, merchants of Big Stone Gap," who probably included several men, "promised to pay monthly sums toward the rent of this room. A number of people have agreed to contribute books and periodicals, others to donate chairs and tables. Mrs. Benedict's idea is to use the room as a rest room for the women and children who come in from the country

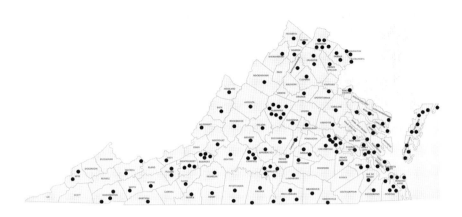

Map of all known ESL chapters, 1917. *Library of Virginia.*

to shop; as a meeting place for the League and the organizations of women who care to use it; and as a library." The mayor authorized policemen to "see to the closing of this library at the proper hour at night and its opening in the morning." Voluntarily or under orders, some men in Big Stone Gap aided the work of local suffragists.[38]

The 1916 annual report for the Williamsburg league contained a lament that some of the most committed local suffragists had moved away but also encouraging news that two new professors at the College of William and Mary supported woman suffrage. In 1917, things looked brighter there. Agnes Foster, who submitted the report that year, recalled that "two or three years ago many of our town women when asked if they would like to join us would laugh nonchalantly even earnestly…& say, 'No indeed.' Today nine women out of ten will reply, 'Yes, I approve most heartily and believe the women should be recognized.'" Foster reported a similar change of opinion among the men. "Two years ago, many of them were offended, as well as indignant, if we asked for their names on any suffrage papers. This winter, those same men, without hesitation, signed our petitions."[39]

Membership in the Equal Suffrage League grew rapidly during the most active period of organizing, from about 1,500 in October 1912 to more than 6,000 by November 1914 and to 9,662 in ninety-eight chapters in eighty-one counties by December 1915. In March 1916, Lila Meade Valentine reported that the approximately 10,000 members made it "larger than any woman's organization in the State" and that it was still "growing daily." Membership reached 13,000 by September 1916, and nearly 16,000 by

December 1917. The many new members in leagues throughout the state and the increased acceptance of woman suffrage that the league promoted also enabled the suffrage cause to make progress with members of the General Assembly. Resolutions to amend the state constitution to allow woman suffrage had failed in 1912 in the House of Delegates by a vote of 12 to 85 and in 1914 by a vote of 13 to 74. It failed again in 1916 but by a margin of only 40 to 52.[40]

At that rate, Virginia suffragists had reason for confidence they could succeed in 1918 or 1920.

5

CONSTANT AGITATION

THE CONGRESSIONAL UNION/NATIONAL WOMAN'S PARTY

The Equal Suffrage League was not the only organization in Virginia that advocated women's right to vote. A small group of the state's suffragists came to believe that an amendment to the Constitution of the United States was the best way to secure voting rights for all women. Instead of having to convince each state legislature to pass a suffrage amendment, a single federal amendment required approval of only three-fourths of the states. In 1912, Mary Morris Hall Lockwood, who lived in the Clarendon section of Alexandria County (Arlington County after 1920), wrote to the Equal Suffrage League of Virginia headquarters hoping to make arrangements for speaking engagements in the area for league president Lila Meade Valentine and novelist Mary Johnston on behalf of an amendment to the state constitution. Less than a year later, however, Lockwood became involved with the nascent Congressional Union for Woman Suffrage on behalf of an amendment to the federal constitution.

Those women endorsed what suffragists usually called the Susan B. Anthony Amendment, which Anthony had drafted in 1875. Section 1, which was almost identical to the language in the Fifteenth Amendment, stated, "The right of citizens of the United States to vote shall not be denied or abridged by the United States or by any State on account of sex." Section 2 borrowed language from the Thirteenth, Fourteenth and Fifteenth Amendments, all of which were deeply unpopular with white political leaders in the South, and declared, "Congress shall have power, by appropriate legislation, to enforce the provisions of this article." In fact, during the 1910s, some southern members of Congress tried to have the Fourteenth and Fifteenth Amendments repealed or have a court declare that they had been ratified improperly and therefore never were part of the Constitution. The prospects for a federal amendment in the South appeared grim.[1]

THE CONGRESSIONAL UNION FOR WOMAN SUFFRAGE

In 1912, Alice Paul took over as chair of the National American Woman Suffrage Association's Congressional Committee and reinvigorated the national campaign for an amendment to the Constitution of the United States. Born into a well-off Quaker family, she grew up on a New Jersey farm where her mother instilled in her a belief in equal rights and woman suffrage. After graduating from Swarthmore in 1905 and earning a master's degree from the University of Pennsylvania in 1907, Paul went to Birmingham, England, to study social work. There, she joined the Women's Social and Political Union, which radical suffragist Emmeline Pankhurst organized in 1903 for aggressively seeking voting rights for all women.

Pankhurst organized protest meetings, demonstrations and marches to Parliament, all of which led to arrests and publicity for the suffrage movement in England. At that time, some English suffragettes, as they were known, were much more radical in their tactics than any American suffragists had been. Paul participated in numerous events and eventually became an organizer. Arrested multiple times, she followed Pankhurst's direction that women demand treatment as political prisoners, who were often granted special status in European countries. When that tactic failed, Paul and other women began hunger strikes. After facing torturous forced feeding, she was released from prison in December 1909 and returned to the United States a month later in poor health.[2]

Paul immediately began planning for a new campaign for woman suffrage in the United States. She was frustrated with the state-by-state campaign but joined the National American Woman Suffrage Association and in 1912 became chair of its Congressional Committee. The committee ostensibly provided an avenue to work with Congress for an amendment to the Constitution of the United States, but it made little headway. As soon as Paul took over, she began organizing a suffrage parade to be held

Alice Paul founded the Congressional Union for Woman Suffrage (later the National Woman's Party) to agitate for an amendment to the Constitution of the United States. *Library of Congress*.

in Washington, D.C., on March 3, 1913, the day before Woodrow Wilson was first inaugurated as president. Paul planned an elaborate procession on Pennsylvania Avenue to draw the attention of the crowds planning to attend the inauguration. The parade, which NAWSA supported, featured a visually dramatic demonstration with numerous floats, bands, mounted brigades and groups of women marching behind banners in color-coordinated attire.

As many as eight thousand women participated in the parade, including more than one hundred Virginians, many of whom belonged to the Equal Suffrage League. Adèle Clark described the enthusiasm of the women who marched behind their white banner with the word *Virginia* in large blue letters. Women, and a few men, from all over the state marched, among them Elizabeth Lewis and her daughter Elizabeth Otey from Lynchburg, Janetta FitzHugh from Fredericksburg, Eugénie Yancey from Bedford, Faith W. Morgan from Newport News and Pauline Adams and Jessie Townsend from Norfolk. Sophie G. Meredith, Kate Langley Bosher and Mary Ellen Pollard Clarke rode in automobiles, while

Thousands of suffragists, including more than one hundred from Virginia, marched in the woman suffrage parade in Washington, D.C., on March 3, 1913. *Library of Congress.*

Mary Johnston marched with the writers. Numerous other Virginians accompanied the different professional groups that included teachers, social workers and businesswomen.

The immense crowds overwhelmed sections of the parade. Clark reported that the Virginians were able to complete their march despite the "outrageous hoodlumism" they experienced during the course of the procession. But Faith Morgan later remembered the "pitiably little protection" the police provided. Not only did some men "spit on or near our skirts," she recalled, but they also stuck out their feet "so as almost to trip us up." Morgan "landed on the next out-projected foot as hard as my 155 lbs would serve me." She concluded with delight, "I could hear a plaintive voice behind me bleating 'she stepped on my foot' 'she stepped on my foot' The glow of my satisfaction is ever burning."[3]

African American women who participated in the parade reported to *The Crisis*, published by the NAACP, that the crowd treated black suffragists no worse than white suffragists. Despite criticism about their participation and being relegated to the back of the parade when some white women threatened to stay away, representatives of the National Association of Colored Women, including founding president Mary Church Terrell, also marched. The founders of the Delta Sigma Theta sorority, which had recently been organized at Howard University to promote academic excellence and public service, were also separated from the white college participants. Undeterred, the young women proudly marched in their caps and gowns. Senior Jimmie B. Bugg, a Lynchburg native, was one of the sorority founders who urged participation in the parade. A few months later, she graduated with honors from Howard's school for teachers and later became dean of girls at a North Carolina high school where she stressed the value of leadership training for girls and women.[4]

The parade and the ineffective police control of the unruly crowd attracted national attention, and Alice Paul planned further demonstrations to keep the proposed federal suffrage amendment in the public eye. Although she endorsed the militant tactics of the English suffragettes, Paul did not express her opinion publicly because she knew that NAWSA did not approve. American suffrage advocates feared being associated with the English women and therefore referred to themselves as suffragists. Paul focused on organizing peaceful events to attract national press coverage.

VIRGINIANS AND THE CONGRESSIONAL UNION

Mary Lockwood eagerly embraced the work of the Congressional Union for Woman Suffrage, which Paul organized in 1913 as a separate organization while remaining chair of NAWSA's Congressional Committee. A Philadelphia native, Lockwood attended a girls' school in North Carolina before she and her husband built Kirkwood, their home in Clarendon, just outside Washington, D.C. She became an ardent advocate for women's rights and social reform and later served a term as president of the Virginia Federation of Women's Clubs. Lockwood also joined the Equal Suffrage League of Virginia but soon began working with the Congressional Union. To combat anti-suffrage assertions that suffragists neglected their "housewifery," she chaired a committee that arranged four days of what a newspaper called "suffrage domestic days" in October 1913 at the former Café Republique in Washington. They prepared dishes using produce from "suffrage gardens" to show that suffragists were capable of taking care of their families. Proving that they were not abandoning their homes while fighting for voting rights was important to suffragists, even though Lockwood and her associates were prosperous white women who had servants to do their housework. In 1912, Lockwood agreed to serve as president of the ladies auxiliary of her church to show that a woman could support suffrage and "remain a churchwoman and still have time to attend to her domestic duties."[5]

When Congress began a special session on April 7, 1913, Lockwood represented Virginia in a demonstration of women from every congressional district. Beginning with speeches at the Columbia Theater, near the White House, the group marched with banners and flags flying and two military bands down Pennsylvania Avenue to the Capitol. A delegation presented petitions in favor of a federal amendment and were seated in the galleries to hear suffrage amendment resolutions introduced in the Senate and the House of Representatives.

By June, Lockwood had taken over as treasurer of the Congressional Union. In her fundraising letters, she argued that the best way to ensure quick passage of a suffrage amendment was "a constant agitation which will rivet the eyes of Congressmen upon our measure." That summer, she helped raise money for an event designed to highlight national support for suffrage after the Senate's Committee on Woman Suffrage had reported favorably on the amendment and placed it on the calendar for discussion. Alice Paul organized women to present to Congress petitions from a quarter of a million suffrists. They gathered on July 31, in Hyattsville, Maryland, to drive in

SUFFRAGISTS' MARCH TO THE CAPITOL, APR. 7, 1913. - #3

On April 7, 1913, Virginia suffragists joined a march to the U.S. Capitol to present suffrage petitions to Congress. *Library of Congress.*

a procession to the Capitol. Lockwood and Pauline Adams both provided automobiles and accompanied the group to Washington with members of the Equal Suffrage Leagues of Alexandria and Norfolk.[6]

Alice Paul had written to leaders of state suffrage organizations in June, including twice to the Equal Suffrage League of Virginia, to request that they participate in the drive to Washington. League president Lila Meade Valentine declined and informed Paul that "there is no movement on foot in Virginia to take part in this demonstration" because the league had previously decided to "take no further action in regard to the National Amendment." Valentine explained that in Virginia an attempt to force "enfranchisement through national action" would be "a grave tactical mistake" and alienate the legislators the suffragists had to persuade. She admitted, however, that she was grateful for the possibility of congressional action because "it gives us a whip hand, as it were, over our Legislature....I am telling the men that Virginia women expect to receive their enfranchisement at an early date from the men of their own state and their own Legislature." She continued her explanation: "There is always danger ahead if justice is too long delayed." Valentine acknowledged that the "stubborn fact we have to face" was that white Virginians feared large numbers of African American women with a ballot. Paul believed that race should not be a factor in supporting a federal amendment and replied to Valentine that "the negro woman's vote can be disposed of the same as that of the negro man's vote."[7]

Valentine identified Pauline Adams as the only local suffrage leader in the state who favored working for a federal amendment, but others such as Lockwood and Sophie Meredith supported it as well. Adams was born in Ireland and immigrated to the United States about 1890. In 1898, she married a Norfolk physician and was almost always thereafter identified in public as Mrs. W.J. Adams. She was an associate editor of the *Jamestown Bulletin*, published by the Woman's Jamestown Association in Norfolk at the time of the Jamestown Ter-Centennial Exposition that commemorated the three hundredth anniversary of the settlement of Virginia. Adams was elected head of the Norfolk Jamestown Esperanto Club in 1906, was a prominent member of the Norfolk Housewives' League and in 1910 was the founding president of the Equal Suffrage League of Norfolk.[8]

Meredith had resided in Richmond since she married a Richmond attorney in 1877. She grew up in Baltimore and in Massachusetts with her Quaker businessman grandfather. Concerned about the condition of public schools in Richmond, Meredith joined the Richmond Education Association, which Lila Meade Valentine and other members of the Woman's Club of Richmond founded in 1900 to work for improvements at schools for white and African American students. From 1906 to 1911, Meredith chaired the association's School Visiting Committee, a group of twenty women who regularly visited the city's schools and called attention to overcrowding, poor facilities and the need to raise teachers' salaries. In 1911, Meredith began a two-year term on the executive committee, although by that time she was focused on securing voting rights for women. Educated to believe in racial and gender equality, she was a founding vice president of the Equal Suffrage League, and like Adams

Sophie Meredith was a founder of the Equal Suffrage League of Virginia and of the Virginia chapter of the Congressional Union for Woman Suffrage in 1915. *Library of Congress*.

and Lockwood, she soon grew frustrated with the slow pace of state-by-state constitutional change and eagerly joined the Congressional Union.[9]

Leaders of the National American Woman Suffrage Association became increasingly concerned about the Congressional Union's demonstrations. A few days before NAWSA's annual convention began in November 1913, members of the union, including Paul and Lockwood, met Emmeline Pankhurst at the railway station in Washington, D.C. Pankhurst had arrived in the United States in October for a speaking tour, although she had been threatened with immediate deportation for moral turpitude as a result of her militant actions in England. Pankhurst spoke in New York and other cities before she arrived in Washington on November 23. NAWSA made it clear that it did not sanction Pankhurst's visit, but the next day she spoke to a packed house at the Columbia Theater about her hunger strikes and the forced feedings she had endured in prison. By then, disagreements between NAWSA and the Congressional Union were so strong that after the NAWSA convention concluded in December, the association removed Paul as chair of the Congressional Committee and expelled the Congressional Union as an affiliate.

LOBBYING CONGRESS

The Congressional Union for Woman Suffrage embraced Pankhurst's strategy in England. Her Women's Social and Political Union had opposed the political party in power if its members did not support woman suffrage. The Congressional Union did likewise because Alice Paul believed that politicians' desire for reelection determined how they voted. Using political pressure and public opinion, she intended to push the issue of women's voting rights and force members of Congress to vote for suffrage if they hoped to hold on to their offices. The Congressional Union focused on events to draw public attention and on intensive lobbying of politicians.

In the spring of 1914, the Senate's Committee on Woman Suffrage favorably reported a federal suffrage amendment, but it failed to pass in the Senate by the required two-thirds majority. Meanwhile, the House of Representatives kept the issue bottled up in committee. The Congressional Union planned simultaneous demonstrations across the country for May 2 in hopes of encouraging Congress to vote for the federal amendment. NAWSA agreed to participate in the effort, and the Equal Suffrage League of Virginia held rallies in Capitol Square in Richmond as well as in Norfolk, Williamsburg and Lynchburg.

A few days later, the Committee on the Judiciary of the House of Representatives reported out the federal amendment with no recommendation, but the Committee on Rules refused to place it on the calendar for consideration and debate. On May 20, 1914, Mary Lockwood, Pauline Adams, Sophie Meredith and others decorated a car with Virginia banners and drove to the Capitol to meet with the chair of the Rules Committee. Their lobbying failed to persuade the Texas Democrat who, like most other southern Democrats, was virulently opposed to woman suffrage. Most or all southern Democrats opposed a federal amendment, which they believed threatened the principle of states' rights and the ability of those states to limit African American voting.

Lucy Burns, a close friend of Paul, coordinated the Congressional Union's lobbying campaign beginning in 1914. She recruited suffragists who came to Washington, D.C., for suffrage events (and even women who were in town on vacation) to meet and educate their legislators. When Maud Younger, a labor activist from California, took over the effort in 1915, the campaign became

In May 1914, Virginia Congressional Union members drove to the U.S. Capitol to meet with the chairman of the Committee on Rules of the House of Representatives. *National Woman's Party.*

more deliberate, with about two dozen women on the job. The CU created index cards on all members of Congress that recorded detailed information on each, including ancestry, education, military service, occupation, religion, hobbies, family members and previous votes on suffrage. When women visited legislators, they added information to the cards, such as remarks legislators made and the men's attitude when addressing the lobbyists. These reports helped the CU hold legislators accountable for their statements and target their efforts.

The Congressional Union also sent organizers out on the road during the summer of 1914 to speak at holiday resorts from the mountains to the beach. They began in the western states—some of which had already granted women the right to vote—and campaigned against Democratic candidates for Congress because the Democratic Party had majorities in both houses of Congress and had not passed the amendment. Early in July, Jessie Hardy Stubbs arrived in Norfolk and made several speeches. Attired in a white dress, the preferred color of the suffragists, she addressed crowds at the steps of the customs building and later at the Ocean View bandstand. Stubbs argued that municipal issues of access to electricity and clean water and milk were also women's issues, and therefore women deserved and needed the right to vote. Confident and composed, she "showed a very admirable sort of bravery" when she began her speech to a very small audience.[10]

The Congressional Union organized state branches across the country. Sophie Meredith formally organized the Virginia branch of the Congressional Union on June 10, 1915. That morning, three cars decorated in the white, gold and purple colors of the Congressional Union stopped in Richmond's business district near Tenth and Main Streets. A crowd of several hundred people heard speeches from several speakers as well as a resolution calling on the city's congressman to support a suffrage amendment. At the elegant Jefferson Hotel, Alice Paul spoke to the founding meeting of the branch. The members elected Meredith chair. Two other early members of the

Congressional Union for Woman Suffrage

VIRGINIA BRANCH

HEADQUARTERS. 204 E. GRACE STREET. RICHMOND, VA.

Congressional Union, Virginia branch, letterhead. *Library of Virginia.*

Equal Suffrage League, Pauline Adams and Elizabeth Otey, were elected vice chairs, as was Dr. Helen Love-Bossieux. The founders elected Marion T. Read secretary and Dorothy Urquhart treasurer. Like the Equal Suffrage League of Virginia, the Congressional Union in Virginia was composed exclusively of white women.

The Equal Suffrage League quickly distanced itself from the Virginia Congressional Union. The headline in a Richmond newspaper article stated, "Women Fall Out Over Suffrage Question." Both organizations made themselves highly visible during the summer and autumn of 1915. In May, even before the formal founding, CU members began holding a series of street meetings on Broad Street in Richmond, near the busy department stores at Fifth and Sixth Streets. Despite having been warned that it was "not safe to speak of the federal amendment, enfranchising women, above a whisper" in Virginia, national organizer Mabel Vernon reported enthusiastic crowds at her June speeches. The Congressional Union and the Equal Suffrage League both held outdoor meetings in the summer in Richmond as well as in Norfolk, Newport News, Hampton, Lynchburg and Warrenton.[11]

Meredith and her allies kept up the pressure on legislators and kept the issue of a federal suffrage amendment in the public eye. Like the Equal Suffrage League, the Virginia Congressional Union had a booth at the state fair in October, where members made speeches throughout the week and passed out literature. The union continued holding street meetings in Richmond in the autumn, and its members met with Virginia senators Claude A. Swanson and Thomas S. Martin, both of whom argued that women did not need the vote to make their voices heard.

The Congressional Union kept steady pressure on congressmen to support a federal amendment, and delegations of women from across the country visited their members of Congress at their offices in Washington and in their districts at home. Virginia women were no different. One week after the Virginia CU was founded in the summer, Pauline Adams led a deputation to speak with Representative Edward E. Holland, a Democrat, of the Second Congressional District, which included Norfolk. She called on him to vote for the amendment to save women "the labor and the tremendous expense" of individual state campaigns and from the "useless indignity" of having to "plead personally with every male voter in this state, no matter how illiterate many of the voters may be, to give women the right to vote in their state." Holland, who had voted against the amendment in January, tried to convince the deputation that he had heard "nothing about suffrage in Virginia," and told them to "make more of a fuss" about the issue. "Just keep at me, and at

The Congressional Union's booth at the Virginia State Fair in October 1916. *National Woman's Party.*

all of us hard enough," he stated prophetically, "and you are bound to win." (Holland nevertheless voted against submission of the amendment to the states in May 1919.)[12]

In July, Mary Lockwood took more than a dozen residents of Alexandria and Fairfax Counties to the office of their congressman, Charles C. Carlin, of the Eighth Congressional District. One woman described herself as a property owner in his district, but she feared she was not protected under the law because she could not vote. Another argued that the women were not looking for "kindness" from the men but "asking for simple justice." Although Lockwood described the continuous growth of suffrage sentiment in his district, Carlin informed them that "in voting against the federal suffrage amendment" he believed he was reflecting his district's opinion. "I feel that the majority of the ladies, as well as the men, are not desirous of suffrage for women in the state of Virginia." The men of Virginia, he condescendingly continued, "have done everything in their power for the ladies," and he incorrectly claimed that Virginia men were among the first

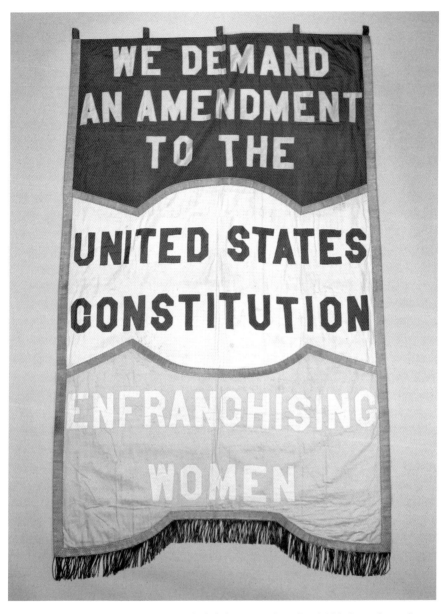

The Congressional Union members took their banners when they lobbied members of Congress for a federal amendment. *Sophie Meredith Sides Cowan.*

in the nation to grant married women full rights to own and dispose of their own property. They were actually among the last to do so, in 1877.[13]

Congressional Union lobbyists faced similar attitudes from most of Virginia's congressional delegation. When Elizabeth Otey drove a group of women to the Appomattox home of Democratic congressman Henry D. Flood in August 1915, her argument that no taxation without representation demanded that woman suffrage be enacted did not sway him. "Even if every man in Virginia wanted the federal amendment," Flood declared, "I would not vote for it." He did not want federal interference in the state control over the franchise, which he feared would destroy white supremacy by allowing more African Americans to vote. Flood expressed disbelief that one of the women, whose family had fought for the Confederacy, could possibly support a federal amendment, but she informed him that she wanted "self-government for women and gaining it as quickly as possible."[14]

Otey and members of the Equal Suffrage League of Lynchburg also visited Representative Carter Glass of the Sixth Congressional District, primary sponsor of the disfranchisement provisions of the Virginia Constitution of 1902. He expressed his opposition to a federal amendment on the grounds that the Fifteenth Amendment had been disastrous for Virginia by allowing African American men to vote. Like the Fifteenth Amendment, the proposed suffrage amendment empowered Congress to enforce it, a power Glass and most other southern politicians dreaded. Otey later remarked that the most significant obstacle suffragists faced in her state was that Virginia politicians "do not honestly believe in democracy. They do not think the people ought to rule."[15]

SHOULDERS TO THE WHEEL

Early in December 1915, senators and representatives again introduced the amendment in both houses of Congress. At the same time, the Congressional Union presented to Congress a massive petition, said to be nearly four miles long and containing half a million signatures. Afterward, one thousand women marched up Pennsylvania Avenue to present it to President Woodrow Wilson at the White House. The Senate again placed the bill on its calendar, but the House of Representatives continued to procrastinate and referred the amendment to its Committee on the Judiciary, where it remained locked up in Charles Carlin's Subcommittee on Constitutional Amendments. In February 1916, the House postponed action until December. Suffragists fought back and succeeded in convincing the judiciary committee to reconsider its decision, but on March 28, Carlin forced a vote to postpone indefinitely consideration of all proposed constitutional amendments, including woman suffrage. Mary Lockwood, Sophie Meredith and other Congressional Union members organized another campaign to highlight the support for woman suffrage in Carlin's northern Virginia district, but he refused to change his mind.

Members of the Congressional Union recruited members and organized new chapters in Virginia. In January 1916, Pauline Adams formed a Norfolk chapter and began work to organize one in nearby Suffolk. State membership chair Julia S. Jennings worked to secure chairs for each of the state's ten congressional districts and hoped to find a chair for each county. Jennings provided the county chairs with lists of members in the vicinity and maps of each district. She grew up on her family farm in Orange County and moved in the 1890s to Richmond, where she worked as a stenographer. Equal Suffrage League officers viewed the work of the Congressional Union as a threat to their own organization. In March 1916, they warned league members that "it is most unwise to divide forces in a cause like ours," and reminded them that it was prepared to lobby for a federal amendment while continuing to advocate a state suffrage amendment.[16]

By the time the Virginia Congressional Union held its annual meeting in June 1916, it had organized six of the state's ten congressional districts, most of them in the eastern half of the state. Meredith praised the dedication of the members but reminded them that "we need money, we need speakers, we need organizers, we need willing workers, we need enthusiasm, self-sacrifice.…I earnestly beg of you each one to put her shoulders to the wheel," she implored them, "to hasten the day when we shall throw off this yoke of slavery and irresponsibility and be able to take our place in the world." Meredith reminded her listeners that they no longer wanted to live in a country of "slavery, injustice and man monopoly," but in a democracy "where all the people, not one-half the people, may make the laws that we must all live under." The Virginia CU experienced its greatest growth then. It increased from 127 members at the end of 1915 to more than 400 during 1916. That, however, was only a small fraction of the Equal Suffrage League's approximately 10,000 members.[17]

The actions of the Democrats who controlled Congress convinced Alice Paul that the party would not support woman suffrage and that it was necessary to continue targeting Democratic candidates in the 1916

Members of the Virginia branch of the Congressional Union greeted Marion Read on her return from the 1916 western states tour. *National Woman's Party*.

election. The Congressional Union proposed to establish a woman's party in several western states, where four million women could vote. A delegation of organizers, including Marion T. Read, the Virginia branch's secretary, headed west on the Suffrage Special train in April to drum up support for a convention to be held in Chicago. When she returned to Richmond on May 18, Congressional Union members met Read at the train station with a fife and drum corps. They drove to Capitol Square, where they held a meeting with a largely male audience.

The Suffrage Special tour helped ensure a large turnout at the national convention in Chicago early in June. More than 1,500 delegates, including Virginia CU membership chair Julia S. Jennings, voted to establish the National Woman's Party. Initially composed of women from the states that had adopted woman suffrage, the party's sole goal was a woman suffrage amendment to the Constitution of the United States. The National Woman's Party hoped to achieve that through a vigorous campaign against President Woodrow Wilson and the national Democratic ticket. The National Woman's Party also convinced Republican presidential nominee Charles Evans Hughes to endorse the amendment, which was the first time a major party's candidate had done so. In another first, the March

1916 state convention of the Republican Party of Virginia, which met in Roanoke, endorsed woman suffrage without expressing a preference for a state or federal amendment. Equal Suffrage League vice president Elizabeth Lewis and local league presidents Nannie Burks and Annie Barna Whitner addressed the convention's Committee on Resolutions, as did Lewis's daughter Elizabeth Otey, who was a vice chair of the Congressional Union in the state.[18]

WE HAVE OUR EYES OPEN TOO

At its August 1916 annual convention, the National Association of Colored Women endorsed Hughes in part as a result of his support for the federal amendment. The convention's resolutions committee, of which Portsmouth resident Josephine Mathews Norcom was a member, also passed a resolution that the federal amendment "granting universal and equal suffrage to all women be urged upon Congress." A native of Wytheville, Norcom graduated from Virginia Normal and Collegiate Institute (later Virginia State University) and lived in Portsmouth with her husband, who was a high school principal. A teacher herself for many years, she was an advocate for social reform, served as secretary of the Woman's Mite Missionary Society in the Virginia conference of the African Methodist Episcopal Church and was a founder of the Virginia State Federation of Colored Women's Clubs. Norcom was chair of the federation committee that recommended establishing the Industrial Home School for Colored Girls that Janie Porter Barrett conducted for many years. Norcom later worked as an executive secretary for the Young Women's Christian Association.[19]

In a 1911 report on African American women's club work, Norcom expounded on the role of women in words that do not significantly differ from words many white suffragists employed to explain their motivations and to win converts. "Man has run life's machine, while woman has furnished the lubricating oil," she began. "Woman thinks not of what she can get but more of what she can give." Norcom described the beneficial work of women's clubs: "Through the club movement we are demonstrating the possibility of women standing on one broad plane of equality, demanding only genuine womanhood as an entrance fee to the great field of service. When one brings this she is not asked if she does manual labor or what kind of work her husband does. We don't care where she sits in the church or whether she sets the style. We ask her to allow her life to conform to the great principles underlying womanhood." To that point in her report, Norcom sounded very much like white club women, but then she specifically addressed the needs and expectations of African American women. "If such a legacy is left to our girls the future of Negro womanhood is assured." Norcom concluded, "The motto of our clubs, 'Lifting as we climb,' is consecrated to the moral, religious, and economic development of ourselves and those around us."[20]

An editorial in the National Association of Colored Women's *National Association Notes* declared in January 1917 that "we, the Negro women, have our eyes open too," and that the association expected its members to fight "unflinchingly" for woman suffrage. Providing an example to refute the argument that women would not vote even if they had the opportunity, some female African American students at Hampton Normal and Agricultural Institute (later Hampton University) participated in a mock presidential election in November 1916, in which Hughes defeated Wilson.[21]

WOMEN ARISE: DEMAND THE VOTE

Throughout the summer and autumn of 1916, Virginia's Congressional Union members visited the state's members of Congress, held public meetings and secured the endorsement of a federal amendment from the Virginia Federation of Labor. Della E. Hooker of Richmond took the federation's resolutions to the White House, but her half-hour conversation with Woodrow Wilson failed to make a dent in his animosity toward the amendment. In October, after Congress had adjourned without taking any action, the Virginia CU again sponsored a booth at the state fair and attracted attention by having nineteen-year-old "Girl Aviator Wonder" Katherine Stinson drop suffrage literature over the midway during one of her daily air show flights.[22]

The Congressional Union strategy of opposing Democratic candidates in 1916 was controversial. The National American Woman Suffrage Association spoke out against it as alienating legislators who were needed to pass any suffrage amendment. The Democrats won majorities in both the Senate and the House of Representatives in November 1916, and Wilson narrowly won reelection. Alice Paul tried to portray the results as favorable to the Congressional Union and National Woman's Party, even though they had not achieved their objectives.

At its annual convention in September 1916, NAWSA debated the future of its work. Some southern women, including Kate Gordon of Louisiana and Laura Clay (sister of Anne Clay Crenshaw, at whose home the Equal Suffrage League of Virginia had been founded) of Kentucky, urged NAWSA to continue working for state suffrage amendments. However, on September 9, delegates approved a resolution that NAWSA "concentrate all its resources" on fighting for a federal amendment. President Carrie Chapman Catt described it as the only self-respecting course to pursue. She asked why American women should have to "beg the vote on bended knee from man to man" and implored them, "Women Arise: Demand the Vote!"[23]

At the Equal Suffrage League of Virginia's annual meeting in November, it revised its strategy to lobby "each congressman and each member of the Legislature, and bring pressure to bear" on them to pass either a state or federal amendment. To refute arguments that the federal government should not interfere with the franchise in the states, the convention also declared that "no constitutional right of a State is abridged" by ratifying a federal amendment through the "method prescribed by the constitution and agreed to by the individual States."[24]

ON THE PICKET LINE AND IN THE PRISON

The Congressional Union increased pressure on Congress and the president. Parades and rallies, cross-country travels and extensive lobbying had boosted awareness and publicity for the proposed federal amendment, but it remained stalled in Congress. To make progress, Alice Paul believed that dramatic public demonstrations would convince politicians that woman suffrage was inevitable. After Woodrow Wilson rejected yet another petition from the Congressional Union, Paul implemented her plan for women to picket the White House "until the passage of the amendment or until the adjournment of Congress."[25]

On January 10, 1917, a group of women left Congressional Union headquarters at Lafayette Square and crossed Pennsylvania Avenue to the White House. There, a dozen women "went on guard" with purple, white and gold banners that displayed the question, "Mr. President What Will You Do For Woman Suffrage?" Six women stood at the east and the west gates of the White House grounds with different picketers rotating throughout the day. Sophie Meredith and Maud Jamison, of Norfolk, took their turns

Among the first pickets outside the White House was Maud Jamison (*fourth from left*), who was arrested more times than any other Virginia suffragist. *Library of Congress.*

among the inaugural group of pickets. Meredith then returned to Richmond to organize members "to hold Virginia Day on picket duty."[26]

More than a dozen Virginia women, including Meredith, Pauline Adams and Julia S. Jennings, traveled overnight by boat and train to Washington, D.C., and spent Saturday, January 27, on the picket line. Women from across the country ignored the cold temperatures, freezing rain and snow to "dramatize for the whole country," as one of them explained, "the women's demand for immediate enfranchisement, and to throw upon the President the responsibility for further delay." Persuading the president to endorse the amendment, Paul believed, would force Congress to act. He had not been convinced through petitions or marches or personal lobbying, so she increased the public pressure on him instead.[27]

Every day suffragists stood at the gates with their banners, through the terrible weather, harassment from passersby and a declaration of war. Paul insisted that the picketing was a nonviolent act and that the picketers were not to respond to insults or abuse. Woodrow Wilson and his White House staff agreed to ignore them, although he did offer to let them stand inside on particularly cold days, which they refused. The pickets attracted a great deal of attention from the press, some of it favorable, some of it unfavorable. An editorial titled "An Absurd Performance" in January 1917 in the *Virginian-*

Pilot and Norfolk Landmark queried whether Wilson could "be influenced by such tactics" and described the picketing as "a silly piece of business, indecorous and presumptive."[28]

The Congressional Union's national convention met at the same time as Wilson's second presidential inauguration in March 1917. At that time, the Congressional Union dissolved into the National Woman's Party, which then became a truly national woman suffrage organization. On the convention's final day, the day before the inauguration ceremony, hundreds of women surrounded the White House with banners and slogans. At least eight Virginians were in the line, standing in the steady rain and wind that "played havoc with the banners."[29]

When the United States entered the First World War in April 1917, the National Woman's Party and the National American Woman Suffrage Association came to different conclusions about the course of action each organization would follow. NAWSA's leaders, even though some of them opposed the war, believed that throwing their support into the war effort rather than the suffrage fight would demonstrate the patriotism of American women and show that they deserved the vote.

Members of the Equal Suffrage League consequently diverted their energy to "every form of war work." Executive Secretary Edith Clark Cowles later

Demonstrators in Washington, D.C., at the time of Woodrow Wilson's second inauguration in March 1917. *Library of Congress.*

reported that "two-thirds of the county chairmen appointed on the Woman's Committee in every drive, were officers and members of the Equal Suffrage League of Virginia." League members served as heads of six departments of the Virginia Women's Committee of the Council of National Defense. Others helped register women as part of food conservation drives, sold war bonds and savings stamps and worked with the Red Cross, the YMCA and other organizations at home and overseas.[30]

The Equal Suffrage League did not abandon the campaign for woman suffrage, and local leagues continued to hold suffrage schools, recruit members and meet with legislators. When the state league moved into more spacious headquarters in September 1917, President Lila Meade Valentine urged women to ask for the vote while helping the war effort "because we wish to have a voice in the Government which we so willingly serve." At the 1918 regular session of the General Assembly, Delegate Holman Willis from Roanoke introduced a resolution to request that Virginia's senators vote for woman suffrage, but the league did not lobby the legislators to pass a state woman suffrage amendment.[31]

Alice Paul, despite knowing that some of her supporters would desert her, decided that the National Woman's Party would continue to battle for a suffrage amendment during the war. She used the party's banners to throw the president's statement of war aims back in his face. Wilson had urged Americans to fight for democracy and the right to have a voice in government. Pickets carried banners with such statements as "Democracy Should Begin at Home" and "We Demand Justice and Self-Government in Our Own Land."[32]

As the picketing continued into the summer, Valentine worried that the increasingly radical tactic would alienate the Virginia men whose votes would be needed to ratify the amendment. On July 2, she issued a press release to condemn "the folly of the fanatical women who are picketing the White House.…We utterly repudiate such methods, and deeply regret that any citizen of the United States should seek to embarrass the President of the government at such a crisis. At the same time, we must protest that it is manifestly unfair and unjust to condemn the suffrage cause as a whole because of the folly of a handful of women."[33]

Woodrow Wilson hoped that ignoring the pickets would make them lose interest and abandon the White House protests, but they did not. When a delegation of Russian diplomats arrived at the White House on June 20, 1917, the pickets embarrassed Wilson with a large banner asking the Russians not to ally with the United States unless American women received the right to vote. Nearby onlookers took offense and attacked the suffragists as treasonous and tore down their banner. That led to even more press coverage and front-page headlines. District of Columbia police began arresting the picketers, ostensibly for obstructing traffic. At first, they were released, but on June 27, six women, including Maud Jamison, were sentenced to pay a fine or serve three days in jail. They refused to pay on the grounds that they were not guilty of any crime and became the first National Woman's Party members in the United States jailed for their suffrage advocacy. A teacher, Jamison had belonged to the Equal Suffrage League of Norfolk until she became secretary of the local chapter of the Congressional Union. She resigned from teaching to work in the headquarters of the National Woman's Party, may have picketed more than any other Virginian and was arrested at least seven times.[34]

The arrests continued through the summer and autumn. Police arrested more than five hundred women during the campaign for woman suffrage, and more than one hundred served jail sentences of a few days to several months; at least three were from Virginia. The arrests were harassment because most of the women broke no laws and did not even block traffic, which was one of the charges. In July, the District of Columbia police court began sending the prisoners to its workhouse located in southern Fairfax County, just across the Occoquan River from the Prince William County town of the same name. As they left the jail, as one woman reported, "a roll of toilet paper was handed to one of the group," as if they could not expect to have any in the workhouse. Workhouse wardens forced the prisoners to remove their clothes, shower in an open space and change into workhouse uniforms. The women described receiving "spoiled and uneatable meat" and "wormy bread." Some of them refused to eat the food. The poor sanitary conditions included shared water buckets for drinking and rats running through the cells. They experienced periods of enforced silence and were often put to work sewing with the other female inmates. Moreover, the suffragists were all white women and were uneasy sharing a dining room and what they called the dormitory with African American prisoners, and they were eventually allowed to eat and sleep separately.[35]

The picketing, arrests and confinements generated unprecedented publicity and may have influenced public opinion in favor of votes for women. The picketers were respectable upper- and middle-class white women of all ages, and the National Woman's Party highlighted the fact that any of them could be anybody's wife, sister, mother or grandmother. "Putting women in jail and in the workhouse will never solve or even help

One of the signs held outside the White House satirized President Woodrow Wilson as "Kaiser Wilson." *Library of Congress.*

the problem," Julia S. Jennings explained to the editor of Richmond's *Evening Journal*, which supported woman suffrage after a new editor replaced an old opponent of votes for women. Woodrow Wilson also understood that picketing would continue until women won the vote. He immediately pardoned the first suffragists who were sent to the workhouse. The district commissioner who supervised the police department, Louis Brownlow, was a future city manager of Petersburg and a supporter of votes for women. He described Wilson as "highly indignant" that the police court had given the women the opportunity to make martyrs of themselves. Despite Wilson's advice against further arrests, Brownlow resolved to police the city as he saw fit to keep peace on Washington's streets during wartime. He feared the "riots" would be used as propaganda in Europe.[36]

In August 1917, Elizabeth Otey joined a protest march to the White House in which she and other women carried banners addressed to "Kaiser Wilson" that referred to the president's wartime expression of sympathy for Germans who had no self-government. The banner stated that "20,000,000 American Women Are Not Self-Governed" and urged the president, "Take The Beam Out Of Your Own Eye." The banners infuriated government workers and military personnel. Some of them blocked the party Otey was in, but other groups made it to the White House. On several occasions during the course of several days, men attacked the suffragists. Police arrested the peaceful picketers, not the men who blocked them, and the violence again generated front-page news coverage.

Later in the month, Pauline Adams, Maud Jamison and Mary Lockwood were all arrested while picketing with banners bearing statements by Wilson. One demanded, "We Cannot Postpone Justice any Longer in These United States." On October 15, while serving their sentences, Adams and the other women then at Occoquan signed a petition to demand that the district commissioners "grant us the rights due political prisoners." They got the petition out of the workhouse by pushing it through pipe openings between their cells. They wanted to draw attention to their treatment as common inmates for having exercised their constitutional rights to assemble peaceably and petition, which were not criminal acts. The commissioners ignored the request and transferred the prisoners to an uninhabited building at the jail in Washington, D.C., where Alice Paul also began serving her own seven-month sentence a few days later. Some of the women, including Adams and Lockwood, appealed their convictions by the police court. After several months of legal wrangling, the District's Court of Appeals ruled on March 4, 1918, that the women had been illegally arrested, convicted and sentenced.[37]

Adams was one of the Virginia women arrested for obstructing traffic and confined to the workhouse for sixty days. Blocking traffic "is the false charge

they trump up against us," she explained in a letter from jail to one of her sons. "There was no one crowding around when I was arrested!" Adams wrote a letter to each of her two sons during her confinement. One is on workhouse stationery; the other is in part on workhouse toilet paper and written a few days before she was released. "I have been kept from the privilege of incoming or outgoing mail for over the past week," she complained in the second letter, "and am now locked in small cell in 'solitary.' I have not been given my tooth brush or hair-brush here yet but got the loan of this pencil from a new picket who came with another group

Tuesday, October 23, '17

W.L.D.C. Jail

Dearest Walter,

Hope everything is all right with you and the home bunch but I have been kept from the privilege of incoming or outgoing mail for over the past week and am now locked in a small cell in "solitary". I have not been given my tooth brush or hair-brush here yet but got the loan of this pencil from a new picket who came with another group yesterday. Two leave tomorrow. They only got 30 days while others have 6 months for doing the same thing "blocking traffic" which is still

Above: In an October 23, 1917 letter to her son, Adams wrote that she was in "solitary" and denied a toothbrush and hairbrush. *Library of Virginia*.

Opposite: Pauline Adams in a replica of her prison garb, 1919. *Library of Congress*.

yesterday." In addition to the suffragists, the workhouse contained women being held for a variety of criminal offenses. Their lot reminded Adams that "drink and drugs are the causes of all the down falls I've seen. And you know men invented them therefore 'Votes for Women.'" To one of her sons she wrote, "Tell Dad that I hope he is not too busy to sometimes think of his 'old lady' 'doing time.'"[38]

While a small number of Virginia National Woman's Party members staffed the White House picket lines, others busily distributed literature, wrote articles for newspapers and interviewed members of Virginia's congressional delegation. They held meetings and organized speaking campaigns around the state. NWP organizer Maud Younger included in her autumn 1917 southern tour speeches in Lynchburg, Petersburg and Richmond, where she and Sophie Meredith met with Governor Henry Carter Stuart. Early in December, Adams and other former inmates at Occoquan spoke about the abuse they suffered to an audience at the Monticello Hotel in Norfolk and to a crowd of seven hundred people on the street. Meredith also called a meeting at the Jefferson Hotel in Richmond, where the Virginia National Woman's Party called for an investigation into inhumane prison conditions.

The National Woman's Party kept stories of the suffragists' treatment before the public, and newspapers around the country responded sympathetically to their plight. In October, the *Evening Journal* editorialized that no matter how much "one may deprecate the picketing tactics," sending Alice Paul and other suffragists to jail on farcical charges of obstructing traffic "is a crime against womanhood, a terrible reflection upon the boasted democracy of the American Republic." Paul began a hunger strike in prison to show her willingness to sacrifice her own body for the suffrage cause. Workhouse officials subjected her to forced feedings through a tube down her throat that caused nose bleeds and vomiting. They kept Paul in solitary confinement and threatened to send her to a mental institution.[39]

To express solidarity with Paul, a group of women picketed the White House again in November. Police arrested them and sent them to the workhouse at Occoquan. After the picketers arrived on the evening of the fourteenth, male guards seized the women (including a Florida woman who was seventy-three years old), dragged them forcibly to a building for male prisoners and hurled them violently into the cells. When the women tried to speak to one another, they were threatened with handcuffs and straightjackets. One suffered heart pains but received no medical attention until the next day. The guards continuously harassed and terrorized the women, some of whom later began hunger strikes and were forcibly fed while being held down. The "Night of Terror" led more newspapers to publish graphic details of the prison conditions and praise the courage of the suffragists.[40]

SO THAT THEY WOULD TAKE NOTICE

The barrage of publicity during the autumn of 1917 may have played a role when in September the House of Representatives created the Committee on Woman Suffrage. This new committee could take action on the issue instead of the recalcitrant Committee on the Judiciary, which had blocked the amendment for months. The Senate's Committee on Woman Suffrage also reported out the amendment favorably that month. The National Woman's Party claimed credit for the progress of the federal amendment, although the National American Woman Suffrage Association continued its own campaigns. Numerous delegates of the Equal Suffrage League of Virginia attended the National American Woman Suffrage Association's annual convention in Washington, D.C., in December 1917. They took the opportunity to meet with Senator Claude A. Swanson, most of Virginia's congressional delegation and congressmen from North and South Carolina. The state's other senator, Thomas S. Martin, exasperated members of the league. "I am quite sure that Virginia does not contain two men," Edith Clark Cowles, the league's executive secretary, later exclaimed, "as rude as Senator Martin." Equal Suffrage League vice president Elizabeth Lewis presented petitions from women across Virginia in support of the suffrage amendment. After visiting individual offices of noncommittal congressmen who agreed only to consider the amendment, Cowles fumed, "If anyone ever again offers me careful consideration I think I shall be tempted to slap his face!"[41]

In January 1918, President Woodrow Wilson informed members of the House suffrage committee that while he preferred that states act on the issue, he advised them to vote in favor of the amendment. On January 10, "with galleries and corridors close-packed with waiting women," the House of Representatives passed the amendment. Despite receiving hundreds of telegrams in support of woman suffrage from Virginians, nine of Virginia's ten representatives voted against the resolution; only C. Bascom Slemp, a Republican from southwestern Virginia, voted in favor.[42]

The confrontational tactics of the National Woman's Party generated national publicity. As Elizabeth Otey explained to the Republican Party state convention in 1920, "We wanted to be disagreeable so that they would take notice." The tactics also drove a wider wedge between the National Woman's Party and the officers of the Equal Suffrage League. Lila Meade Valentine and some other officers generally refrained from public criticism of Virginians who participated in the demonstrations in Washington, but they believed that the NWP made it more difficult to win converts in Virginia and blamed the party's national leaders. "If only Alice Paul could be kept quiet for a while," Valentine grumbled privately early in 1918, "we might get something accomplished."[43]

Virginia women went to work immediately after the House vote to convince the state's senators to vote for the amendment. National Woman's Party organizers spoke in Big Stone Gap, Charlottesville, Lynchburg, Newport News, Norfolk, Richmond and Roanoke. The Virginia members continued to lobby Senators Martin and Swanson. At a January 28, 1918 meeting of the state committee of the National Woman's Party in Richmond, Alice Paul urged her allies to wage a vigorous political campaign against both senators. At the annual meeting in April, vice chair Helen Love-Bossieux reported sending 150 letters and 47 telegrams to politicians. Members applauded when president Sophie Meredith told them that they needed to put aside personal business until Congress passed the amendment.

Equal Suffrage League members were active, too. They traveled and spoke on behalf of woman suffrage, and the league's legislative committee lobbied Virginia senators to support the amendment. The league also decorated a suffrage float for a thrift stamp parade in Richmond in March 1918. Ralph Wormeley, fourteen-year-old-son of Richmond suffragist Sarah Blair Harvie Wormeley, dressed as Uncle Sam and rode on the float. He also joined the Equal Suffrage League.

With the Senate about to recess without having voted on the amendment, the National Woman's Party protested in Lafayette Square across the street from the White House. On August 6, 1918, police arrested four dozen women as they tried to make speeches at the base of the statue of the Marquis de Lafayette. To the alarm of her friends, Sophie Meredith, "our frail but fearless chairman," was among those arrested "while performing her duty in protesting against the delay." At age sixty-six, she was one of the oldest women arrested and bowed to her family's belief that a live suffragist was better than a dead one and paid her fine instead of going to prison. She was fortunate. On this occasion, the women were jailed in an abandoned

The Equal Suffrage League float in the 1918 thrift stamp parade in Richmond. Ida Mae Thompson (*left*) and Edith Clark Cowles hold the banner. *VCU Libraries.*

I BELIEVE IN EQUAL SUFFRAGE FOR MEN AND WOMEN, AND I HEREBY ENROLL MYSELF AS A MEMBER OF THE EQUAL SUFFRAGE LEAGUE.

Ralph Wormeley
102 W. Grace St.
Richmond Va.,

STATE HEADQUARTERS, RICHMOND, VA.
Commercial Building, Second Street, between Broad and Grace.

NO DUES
DATE: *June 8, 1915*

Ralph Wormeley, son of suffragist Sarah Wormeley, dutifully paid his dues to join the Equal Suffrage League. *Library of Virginia.*

building deemed uninhabitable at the city's prison complex. The cells were dark and damp with open drains and toilets and straw pallets on iron cots. The foul smell and dirty drinking water left them ill, and some women again went on hunger strikes. Protests against the poor conditions led to their early release after just five days, and authorities granted permission for a subsequent planned demonstration.[44]

Demonstrations continued into September 1918. The National Woman's Party burned copies of President Woodrow Wilson's wartime speeches on democracy at the base of the Lafayette statue to highlight his hypocrisy. On the last day of the month, the president made a personal appeal to the Senate. If the United States wished "to lead the world to democracy," he told the senators on the floor and the crowds in the galleries, the country had to demonstrate its own commitment. Wilson had at last concluded that extending the franchise to women was "vitally essential to the successful prosecution of the great war of humanity in which we are engaged." It was not enough. The Senate failed to approve the amendment by two votes.[45]

Decrying "Autocracy at Home," the National Woman's Party shifted its focus to the "Thirty-Four Wilful Men," including both Virginia senators, who had voted against the amendment. On October 7, 1918, pickets began a month of demonstrations at the Capitol in Washington. Police confiscated their banners and detained the women in the guard room (but did not arrest them) until the Senate had adjourned for the day. Police pushed the women against the walls or threw them to the floor while dragging them away. Maud Jamison declared that "such brutality" by the Capitol police was "an intolerable insult to all the women of the nation." With five open Senate seats up for election in November, the National Woman's Party also campaigned for suffrage supporters and helped secure a slim Republican majority in the Senate.[46]

The Sixty-Fifth Congress convened for its final, short session on December 2, 1918, less than a month after the end of the world war. In his annual address, Woodrow Wilson paid tribute to the contributions of women to the American war effort. He called on Congress to "make them the equals of men in political rights." Alice Paul was disappointed that Wilson immediately left for France to attend the preliminary peace conference and did not remain in Washington to keep up the momentum for suffrage, and she revived the "watchfires of freedom." On January 1, 1919, National Woman's Party members again began burning copies of Wilson's speeches to highlight his obstruction of democracy at home. Groups of women guarded the flame each night despite numerous arrests and police attempts to extinguish it.[47]

In February 1919, Norfolk resident Nell Mercer was arrested with other members of the National Woman's Party and sentenced to five days in jail. *Library of Congress.*

On February 9, the NWP staged one of its most dramatic demonstrations when one hundred women marched to the White House with banners, the watchfire urn and an effigy of Woodrow Wilson that they proceeded to burn. Half a dozen Virginians participated, including Nell Mercer, who helped carry the urn, and Pauline Adams, who carried a banner that asked why Wilson could not secure the necessary votes from members of his own party. Arrested again, Adams escaped conviction for lack of evidence. Mercer was sentenced to five days in prison. Despite their efforts, the Senate narrowly defeated the suffrage amendment that month.

In a last-ditch attempt to persuade senators to approve suffrage before the end of the Sixty-Fifth Congress, National Woman's Party leaders raised about $20,000 (Sophie Meredith pledged $400) to hire a train and send a group of former workhouse prisoners on a national tour they called the Prison Special. Adams was one of almost two dozen women who left Washington, D.C., by train on February 15, 1919, and headed across the country. At each stop,

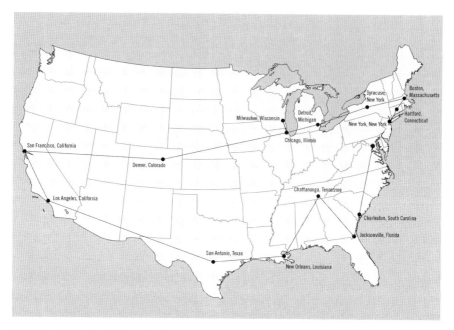

In 1919, the National Woman's Party sponsored a Prison Special to take former imprisoned suffragists around the country. *Library of Virginia.*

former prisoners clad in replicas of their prison attire shared their stories of protest and mistreatment. The political chair of the National Woman's Party explained, "We intend to make it clear to the people of the country that the Administration is responsible for the fact that American women are forced to endure imprisonment in their effort to secure the passage of the amendment." The Prison Special returned on March 11, the women having shown their mettle and resolve to keep fighting until Congress approved an amendment to grant the vote for all American women.[48]

AN ELEMENT OF DISCORD

Racial prejudice continued to complicate the work of suffragists in Virginia and in Washington. Early in 1919, when the Northeastern Federation of Colored Women's Clubs proposed affiliating with the National American Woman Suffrage Association, Lila Meade Valentine advised against the move because it "would materially cripple the work" of NAWSA "in the

South." Valentine privately explained to one NAWSA officer, "I believe that all women, white or black, who meet the qualifications for suffrage in any State should have that right, but in working to secure that right, we should exercise common sense, and not complicate our efforts and add to the difficulties of the task by injecting elements of discord. As you know, the negro is the one remaining argument against suffrage in the Southern States and our work in behalf of the federal amendment, already meeting great opposition because of that element, would be rendered immeasurably more difficult by admitting a large body of negro women to membership in the National at this time. This is not a matter of principle but of expediency."[49]

As Valentine explained, the proposed amendment to the federal constitution offended many southern politicians who still resented the Fifteenth Amendment, which granted the vote to African American men and empowered Congress to enforce it. Those politicians were devoted to white supremacy and used the doctrine of states' rights to oppose the federal amendment. That so exasperated Jessie Townsend, whose concern was with women's rights, that in June 1918 she telegraphed Senator Claude A. Swanson, "We await your decision whether state rights or our rights."[50]

CONGRESS PASSES THE AMENDMENT

Congress adjourned on March 4, 1919. That meant the suffragists would have to wait until the next Congress began in December. Fortunately for suffrage advocates, the president called a special session to pass an appropriations bill to fund government operations. The Sixty-Sixth Congress opened with new Republican majorities in both houses on May 19, 1919. In his message sent from France, Wilson commended the "steadfast courage" of women who had long advocated the amendment and urged its "immediate adoption." On May 21, the House of Representatives approved the amendment by a large majority, 304 to 89, with Virginia's members all voting against except Republican C. Bascom Slemp. On June 4, the Senate passed the amendment by a vote of 56 to 25, slightly more than the required two-thirds majority. Virginia was one of only eight states (six of them in the South) whose two senators both opposed the amendment. Equal Suffrage League members had inundated the state's congressional delegation with letters and telegrams to no avail, and after their negative votes the league followed up with a public letter to protest their "persistent unfriendliness to the enfranchisement of women." The *Evening Journal* denounced the delegation's opposition as a "sorry position to take and wholly untenable."[51]

Equal Suffrage League president Lila Meade Valentine rejoiced that Congress had at last taken action, although she regretted that Virginia "did not long ago take the initiative" by passing a state amendment. "I trust," Valentine concluded, that the General Assembly "may atone for the past neglect by being among the first to ratify the national amendment." Nora Houston, secretary of the Equal Suffrage League of Richmond, hoped "that the forces of democracy will never be turned back again"; Adèle Clark called on the men of Virginia to "prove their political kinship" with George Washington, Thomas Jefferson and Patrick Henry by quickly ratifying the amendment; but Lucy Randolph Mason, president of the Richmond league, realistically predicted that it might take a few years for enough states to ratify it.[52]

DIFFERENCES AMONG VIRGINIA SUFFRAGISTS

Leaders of the Equal Suffrage League and the National Woman's Party in the state grew further and further apart during the campaign for woman suffrage in Virginia. They shared the same goal of winning the right to vote, but their different strategies of pursuing that goal at the state and national levels and their different tactics of persuasion and confrontation revealed or created differences in temperament and outlook and led them to take different political paths then and after they won the vote.

Lila Meade Valentine, Jessie Townsend, Elizabeth Lewis, Adèle Clark and most other league officers believed in persuasion and were uncomfortable with confrontation. They easily conformed to venerable gender conventions that allowed them to make their case for woman suffrage, but they eschewed confrontational politics, and most of them avoided public criticism of people who differed with them. They understood that the culture in which they lived gave them a chance to reach their goal so long as they did not significantly transgress the acceptable code of conduct for white ladies in Virginia. It should have been no surprise that they were inclined to join the Virginia League of Women Voters, which was founded late in 1920, rather than support the more radical goals of women who in the 1920s favored an Equal Rights Amendment to the Constitution of the United States to guarantee full gender equality. And it should be no surprise that they correctly predicted that Virginia's white male politicians would not vote for an amendment to the federal constitution that granted all women the right to vote but that they might eventually vote for an amendment to the state constitution that achieved that same purpose for Virginia women.

Sophie Meredith, Mary Lockwood, Pauline Adams and the other women who signed on early in favor of a federal suffrage amendment worked within a national political context and for the most part with a national audience. They acted more boldly, either from natural inclination or from necessity. Perhaps because some of them had grown up elsewhere, they imposed fewer restraints on themselves than most native Virginia women did. And even among the natives of Virginia, a woman like Elizabeth Otey—who had a rigorous academic education at Bryn Mawr, the University of Chicago and the University of Berlin—may have been more at ease with bold political action. They more readily embraced more radical gender politics in and after their participation in the suffrage movement and endorsed the proposed Equal Rights Amendment first introduced in Congress in 1923. It should not be surprising that they believed or came to believe that their provocative style would create sympathy when their opponents harassed or jailed them. It may also be no surprise that, unlike leaders of the Equal Suffrage League, they misread the state's political culture and believed that it was possible to persuade or force the General Assembly to ratify the Nineteenth Amendment.

A DETERMINED AND AGGRESSIVE LOBBY

SUCCESS IN 1920

S usie A. Shepperson grew up in her native Chesterfield County during the suffrage movement in the 1910s and attended the senior high school at Virginia Normal and Industrial Institute (later Virginia State University) before she began a career as a public school teacher. She won a national prize in 1919 for the best essay on the subject "Does the European War Present Any Future Economic, Social, or Political Advantages to the Negro Race?" Early in 1920, the institute's *Gazette* printed her prizewinning essay. The United States, Shepperson explained, entered the war in "a heroic stand for democracy, for liberty and right." African Americans understood that their sacrifices on the battlefield and on the homefront together with the migration of many working people from the South to manufacturing jobs in the North changed the country and created new opportunities for them. Among those changes, Shepperson believed that the "great woman suffrage movement" had convinced millions of men "that women should be allowed to exercise every political right extended to ma[l]e citizens of this country." In fact, "Negro suffrage and woman suffrage are insolubly bound together," and a "greater political interest has been created by the war, and the Negro has caught the spirit." Shepperson predicted that African Americans, both women and men, would finally become full political citizens.[1]

The long campaign for woman suffrage and the rhetoric of liberty and democracy during the First World War, as Shepperson's essay demonstrated, altered the context of public debate on woman suffrage by June 1919 when Congress submitted the proposed amendment to the states for ratification.

SPECIAL SESSION OF THE GENERAL ASSEMBLY, AUGUST–SEPTEMBER 1919

Members of the National Woman's Party and of the Equal Suffrage League focused their attentions back on the General Assembly of Virginia, which was not scheduled to meet again in regular session until January 1920. The National Woman's Party began its ratification campaign immediately. Armed with a large map of the state, national organizer Anita Pollitzer went "scooting across the country," from the Eastern Shore to central Virginia. Spending long hot days traveling by train and car, Pollitzer attempted to convince legislators to take this opportunity to ratify the amendment. The president of the Equal Suffrage League of Williamsburg placed a large map of the United States in the courthouse of James City County and kept track of progress by adding a new star for each state that ratified the amendment.[2]

In the meantime, though, the governor called for a special session of the assembly to meet in mid-August 1919 to prepare a plan for taking advantage of a federal grant for construction of public roads. Pollitzer and two other organizers joined Sophie Meredith, Elizabeth Otey, Pauline Adams and others who lobbied legislators to ratify the amendment. The Equal Suffrage League's officers wished to prepare more thoroughly for the January 1920 regular session and not risk alienating legislators or jeopardizing ratification by introducing the subject of woman suffrage in the special session. Lila Meade Valentine and the other officers feared that the confrontational tactics of the National Woman's Party would doom their cause in the special session.

Elizabeth Otey and her mother, Elizabeth Lewis, who was then briefly acting president of the Equal Suffrage League, joined the league's officers and lobbyists in Murphy's Hotel in Richmond, where many members of the General Assembly stayed during the special session. By then, Otey was widely recognized as one of the National Woman's Party radicals. Adèle Clark and other league leaders privately complained to Carrie Chapman Catt about the problems they faced. "Naturally," Edith Clark Cowles explained in a postscript to Clark's letter to Catt, "Mrs. Otey's presence has somewhat complicated matters, greatly confusing us with the Woman's Party in the minds of some of the men." Privately, Cowles explained to an officer of the Williamsburg league, "Our ratification committee has been having all sorts of trouble with the methods of the Woman's Party. They have been at the Capitol in full force, and haven't failed to antagonize

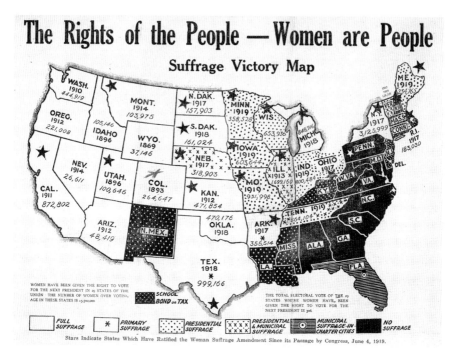

Throughout their campaigns, suffragists displayed maps to show where women could—and could not—vote. *Library of Congress.*

each man they interviewed to such an extent that when our committee approached the same man for our own poll, they first had to smooth him down." Cowles mentioned that Norvell L. Henley, who represented Williamsburg in the House of Delegates, "told one of our workers that if he had not been so strong a suffragist, that Mrs. Meredith would have made an anti out of him, or words to that effect. It is very disheartening, but it looks as though we had to endure it."[3]

The governor submitted the amendment to the General Assembly, and a week into the session, Woodrow Wilson sent telegrams to the president pro tem of the Virginia Senate and to the Speaker of the House of Delegates urging "the Legislature of my native state" to adopt this amendment "of profound importance to our country." Meredith, Otey, Adams and officers and members of the National Woman's Party helped persuade sympathetic members of both houses to introduce resolutions to ratify the amendment. As officers of the league feared, the move failed, and as all suffragists dreaded, the specter of African American voting loomed large over the proceedings. One Alabama association telegraphed the Virginia assembly to urge rejection of the amendment. The Alabamians feared that if Virginians ratified the amendment, "there is no hope, no help nor justice," and they might as well "tear down your Confederate monuments."[4]

At the beginning of September, Delegate Thomas Ozlin of Lunenburg County and Senator Robert F. Leedy, who represented the district that included Clarke, Page and Warren Counties, introduced resolutions that condemned the federal amendment. On September 3, the House of Delegates by a vote of 61 to 21 passed Ozlin's resolution that denounced the amendment as "an unwarranted, unnecessary, undemocratic and dangerous interference with the rights reserved to the States or to the people in both State and Federal Constitutions." The next day, the House of Delegates refused by a vote of 50 to 17 to rescind the resolution, and the Senate voted 19 to 14 "to pass the resolution by indefinitely," meaning that the senators would not take up the subject again. That concluded the assembly's action on the amendment in the special session and postponed further consideration until the January 1920 regular session.[5]

ENROLLING SUPPORTERS OF WOMAN SUFFRAGE

The National Woman's Party and the Equal Suffrage League continued their work right up to the last minute. In anticipation of the November 1919 election, when voters would elect all forty members of the Senate and all one hundred members of the House of Delegates, the league's leaders began their most ambitious project. In 1918 and 1919, they conducted a campaign to enroll as many supporters of woman suffrage in each county and city as the number of men who had voted in each in a recent election. It is unclear to which election they referred, but in the 1917 gubernatorial election, 89,862 men had voted. League leaders even hoped to reach a quarter million supporters. The goal was to persuade members of the General Assembly that a great many Virginia women really did want the vote, that an increasing number of men approved of woman suffrage and that legislators who voted against woman suffrage would not likely receive the votes of those men or of the women when they were finally able to vote.

Several times during that part of the campaign, Equal Suffrage League president Lila Meade Valentine had to stop working because of her illness or the poor health of her husband, who also was a member of the league and heartily endorsed her tireless work for the cause. He suffered from heart disease and other afflictions off and on for several years. They traveled to the warmer South early in 1917 for several weeks and later that spring to Baltimore, where he spent time in a hospital. In the spring of 1918, they returned to Baltimore where she had a major operation and did not resume work in Richmond until the autumn. Valentine was down with a serious case of influenza in the spring of 1919. Her husband died suddenly on June 10, 1919, which caused the league to cancel a planned celebration of congressional passage of the proposed amendment. She spent most of the remainder of the summer in Maine recovering from the shock. Valentine was back in the office, though, dictating and writing letters late in August and overseeing strategy for the special session of the General Assembly that met then. She also suffered another prolonged and debilitating attack of influenza early in 1920.

League vice presidents Elizabeth Lewis (Lynchburg), Jessie Townsend (Norfolk), Faith Morgan (Newport News) and Kate Langley Bosher (Richmond) stepped up during Valentine's absences and illnesses and provided experienced direction for the league. Adèle Clark also assumed an expanded leadership role during that time and worked closely with the league's officers. The small and talented office staff Valentine had recruited—Ida Mae Thompson and Edith Clark Cowles in particular—acted more or less as full equal partners with the league's vice presidents during Valentine's absences. Together, they guided the organization and directed the work of its local leagues and the women who canvassed to enroll supporters before the 1920 session of the General Assembly. This unusual collegial leadership was one of the strengths of the Equal Suffrage League.

Morgan did a great deal of the enrollment work herself. She traveled alone most of the time and at her own personal expense. Morgan depended on railroads because she did not drive. She spent weeks at a time in towns and cities in the northern and southern parts of Virginia and in the Shenandoah Valley. Morgan planned her work to achieve maximum results by going to towns with enough hotel rooms or boarding places she could use as bases of operations. Not a comfortable or particularly able public speaker, she was most effective in small groups and did her best work going door-to-door. The pace was slow and labor intensive. Morgan sought out men and women of social influence, including ministers and teachers, to sign her petitions, preferably at the top of the page, to encourage other people to sign below their names. When Cowles later wrote the Virginia chapter for the 1922 volume in the *History of Woman Suffrage* series, she singled out Morgan for special commendation: "The enrollment of 32,000 men and women was accomplished in 1919, Mrs. Faith W. Morgan, a vice-president of the association, securing the largest number of names."[6]

In that volume, Cowles also gave Morgan's former neighbor Ellen Robinson a small measure of immortality for her work enrolling supporters. Robinson moved to Strasburg, in Shenandoah County, late in the decade to care for her widowed, terminally ill mother and from 1918 to 1920 did much less work for woman suffrage than before. Nevertheless, she scoured Shenandoah County in 1919 and obtained her quota of signatures earlier than any other person in the state. It was a small quota, Robinson acknowledged, but "it meant a great deal in this hard field & 150 here is equal to 1000 in some places."[7]

Mary Elizabeth Pidgeon, a Quaker and Clarke County native, joined the campaign to enroll suffrage supporters in December 1918.

Mary Elizabeth Pidgeon worked for woman suffrage in New York, South Dakota, North Carolina and Virginia from 1917 to 1920. *Bryn Mawr College, Special Collections.*

She had taught in a Quaker school in Pennsylvania from 1914 to 1917 but took part in suffrage events earlier in the decade while still in college. In 1917, Pidgeon quit teaching to work in New York as a paid field organizer for the National American Woman Suffrage Association, as Eudora Ramsay had been. After New York women won the right to vote later that year, the association sent her to South Dakota. Pidgeon made speeches, lobbied politicians and organized for the South Dakota Universal Franchise League. Women won the right to vote there in a referendum in November 1918.[8]

NAWSA then sent Pidgeon to her native Virginia to assist in enrolling supporters. She worked first in the northern counties near where she had grown up, but she also worked in Portsmouth and in Norfolk, where she enrolled more than one thousand supporters. She made an extended trip in the summer of 1919 to sign up women in the area between Bristol and Roanoke. Except for a brief mission to North Carolina in the hottest part of that summer, Pidgeon worked in Virginia until the spring of 1920. Several times a week, she wrote and sent to officers of the league detailed reports of her progress, including lists of men and women to be cultivated as future supporters. An energetic and capable canvasser, Pidgeon signed up a great many Virginians in support of votes for women, even in Pulaski County, where early organizational work had failed to bear much fruit. Her work with Annie B. Whitner and other suffragists in and around Roanoke was particularly successful. "The Roanoke League has outstripped everything in Virginia," Ida Mae Thompson reported to Valentine early in July 1919, "and wound up its enrollment campaign with a big jubilee meeting at Mrs. Whitner's home. Over 2200 women were enrolled!!!"[9]

Pidgeon wrote some of the first of her many long and detailed field reports in Virginia on stationery of the South Dakota Universal Franchise League that she saved after the conclusion of her work in that state. She sometimes carried away handfuls of hotel stationery for writing reports, saving herself and the league the small expense of purchasing paper. Pidgeon also wrote an article titled "From the Virginia Battle Front" for the February 21, 1920 issue of the national journal the *Woman Citizen*, on the work she and other suffragists were doing in Virginia. She quickly earned the respect of the league's state officers and became close friends with Thompson, Cowles and Clark in the Richmond office. In the summer of 1919, Pidgeon even began informally and unconventionally addressing her letters to Cowles "Dear Edith," and in the autumn Cowles reciprocated with "Dear Elizabeth." Pidgeon also addressed Adèle Clark once as "Dear Adèle." Pidgeon's letters to Carrie Chapman Catt, Lila Meade Valentine and other NAWSA and league officers, however, though witty, detailed and anecdotal in content, were always formal and correct in style.

By the time the Equal Suffrage League concluded the enrollment campaign in 1919, its members had signed up 32,000 supporters of woman suffrage. That was far short of the hoped-for 250,000, but with a statewide membership then of 20,000 or more, the league was stronger than it had ever been.[10]

THE ELECTION OF 1919

The work of the suffragists together with several other unrelated events significantly changed the political dynamics in Virginia by the opening of the 1920 regular session of the General Assembly, which would again consider the proposed Nineteenth Amendment. The dominant Democratic Party remained badly divided as a result of years of internal conflicts about prohibition, the party's leadership and the bitter 1917 gubernatorial primary. The three candidates that year included two opponents of the party leadership, suffrage supporter John Garland Pollard and a newcomer to state politics, Westmoreland Davis. The incumbent lieutenant governor, J. Taylor Ellyson, was a regular party man. The three also included two prohibitionists, Pollard and Ellyson. Davis tried to remain neutral on the controversial issue of prohibition and received most of the votes of men who opposed prohibition. Davis won the nomination and the general election in November 1917. As party leaders Senators Thomas S. Martin and Claude A. Swanson feared, Davis began making plans to challenge their leadership.

In that complex and continuously changing political context, nearly half of the legislators who were in office when the special session of the General Assembly refused to ratify the Nineteenth Amendment early in September 1919 were not even on the ballot in the November general election. It is not clear whether the issue of woman suffrage and the increased support it had gained in Virginia played a significant role in the large turnover of membership in both the Senate and the House of Delegates. An editorial in the *Richmond Times-Dispatch* characterized the August 5, 1919 Democratic Party primary as "devoid of issues," but differences among Democrats about the party's leadership, prohibition, woman suffrage and proposals to issue bonds to speed construction of public roads could all have contributed to a large number of Democratic legislators who retired or failed to win renomination.[11]

The November 1919 general election brought eighteen new members into the forty-member Senate and fifty-seven new members into the one-hundred-member House of Delegates. Five more delegates who won election in November were almost new, having been elected to fill vacant seats after the 1917 election. "There are but 20 Republicans in the entire General Assembly of 140 men," Valentine informed Carrie Chapman Catt early in 1920. "Fourteen in the House and six in the Senate, a gain of two members over last session in the House and one in the Senate, a negligible factor in either body as far as changing the sentiment is concerned." She may not have perceived the potential importance of the replacement of a large number of Democrats with other Democrats.[12]

Following Martin's sudden death a few days after the 1919 election, Davis appointed Secretary of the Treasury Carter Glass, a former Virginia congressman, to the vacant Senate seat. Glass was a longtime opponent of Martin and Swanson and appeared to be the ideal ally for Davis in seizing control of the party. However, Glass quickly made peace with Swanson so as to have no serious opposition when he ran in a November 1920 special election for the remainder of the term to which Martin had been elected in 1918. Consulting his political future further, Glass came out in favor of woman suffrage early in 1920. Elizabeth Lewis, Elizabeth Otey and other suffragists in Glass's hometown of Lynchburg had never been able to get a commitment from him when they asked if he favored woman suffrage, which they correctly surmised meant that he did not. Glass, in fact, was publisher of one of the Lynchburg newspapers that Lewis had once characterized as "democratic (?)" but opposed to the democratic reform of granting women the vote. In 1920, it was not in the interest of the new senator to alienate potential new voters on the eve of his statewide campaign.[13]

Glass was not the only Virginia politician who became convinced by 1920 that woman suffrage was not a bad thing or that it was going to be adopted sooner or later and that he had better not displease future voters. At the beginning of February 1920, even Charles Carlin, who had bottled up the proposed Nineteenth Amendment in a subcommittee of the House of Representatives before he retired from Congress, came around. He had maintained for years that most Virginia women did not want to vote, but he could clearly see the conspicuous support for woman suffrage in the state and changed his mind. "I am now convinced that they do want the right to vote," Carlin announced, "and am further convinced that they ought to have it." He believed that the state constitution permitted the General Assembly to grant women the vote, an interpretation almost nobody else agreed with and which was almost certainly incorrect. "Let's give it to them ourselves," Carlin concluded, "let's give it to them now, let those of us who have heretofore stood in bold opposition bow gracefully to the inevitable and graciously surrender to the wishes of our own women rather than grudgingly submit to the determined purposes of those of other States."[14]

POLLING THE POLITICIANS

In final preparation for the 1919 primary and general election, officers in the Equal Suffrage League headquarters compiled data on members of the House of Delegates, including polling them before the special session about whether to bring up the proposed Nineteenth Amendment then. For nearly every member and for most of the new members elected in November, they recorded on index cards all that they could learn about legislators' positions on woman suffrage. This important lobbying work resembled the National Woman's Party compilation of records of senators and congressmen and might have been an innovation in Virginia. They filed the cards alphabetically in a pasteboard box. League officers sent each legislator a questionnaire and a letter from Valentine and also interviewed most of the reelected and newly elected legislators. Mary Elizabeth Pidgeon, Eugenia Jobson, Nora Houston and Adèle Clark conducted most of the interviews. They also returned to speak to many of the legislators during the 1920 session of the General Assembly.[15]

They interviewed the state senators and may have prepared cards for them, too, but no cards for senators are preserved in the league's records. Pidgeon's reports from northwestern Virginia, for instance, include several accounts of interviews with Harry Flood Byrd, the recently reelected member of the Senate from the district that included Winchester. In January, a delegation of local suffragists interviewed him. "He told them," as they related the conversation, "he was prejudiced against suffrage. If he had not been prejudiced, he could not support it anyway because he believed it would permit negro women to vote without qualification until the Va. constitution was amended. Enrollment had little weight" with him. Attached to the report is a transcription of a December 4, 1919 letter from Byrd to a member of the committee in which he wrote, "If the situation is in Virginia as I understand it—namely, that negro women can vote in Virginia without even an educational or poll tax requirement until the Constitution is amended, I feel certain that a large majority of the women of this state would not favor women suffrage." Next to that passage, somebody wrote in the margin, "Even after Mrs Valentine's explanation" that all new voters would have to register under the existing severely restrictive laws in force in the state.[16]

As Valentine had recently explained to Pidgeon, "the antis are simply putting up the negro woman as bogey. The negro woman is no more of a menace than is the negro man. White supremacy is maintained in both cases by the restrictions imposed by each State Constitution. It goes without saying that each State Legislature will take all necessary steps to make these restrictions apply to the woman voter when the federal amendment is ratified. That is all that we need say."[17]

Many of the cards for members of the House of Delegates included an estimation of the likelihood that the delegate would support woman suffrage. Two reported that delegates were "Turnable," or open to persuasion. Cards for legislators from western counties contained notes from "M.E.P.'s list Mountain Counties," an analysis or list that Pidgeon compiled of delegates' and senators' stances on woman suffrage. The original list is evidently lost, but several of her reports contained information about those legislators.

Some of the cards record Pidgeon's vague notation, "Favorably doubtful," by which she may have meant that those legislators were, for one reason or another, like Glass and Carlin, "Turnable."

A note on the card for Richmond delegate Albert Orlando Brown included the word *Negrophobia*, which indicated that he feared that extending the vote to women would mean more and dangerous African American voting. Mayo C. Brown from Lynchburg told interviewers that he was "not opposed to suffrage but not enthusiastic and will vote against Ratification." On the card for Samuel R. Carter, a new delegate from Ashland, is the note, "Shall be guided by his wife's wishes. Mrs C. opposed." Eugenia Jobson showed E. Griffith Dodson, who won reelection in Norfolk in 1919, petitions in favor of woman suffrage from people in his district. She recorded, "The more he was talked to about it the more determined he became against. no women in his family wanted it." Dodson "Ignored petitions." A new delegate from Culpeper County, Edwin H. Gibson, was "Not in position to commit himself. In quandary. Approves suffrage. Must represent constituents" whom he evidently believed did not approve but "does not want to take a stand against suffrage." The card also recorded that the Culpeper County delegate "said he was in favor of suffrage but not the Federal amendment. As for his vote is undecided. His wife is a suffragist and on Ratification committee and is said to have more influence with him than anybody else." Therefore, somebody in the state office wrote at the bottom, "Turnable."

Nora Houston and Elizabeth Lewis both learned from people in Louisa County that the delegate from that county, R. Lindsay Gordon, would vote for suffrage, and they recorded that he wrote on December 15, "Can count on me to do all I can for the cause. Thinks Gov.'s help important." Several notes are on the card for M.E. Padgett, a new member from Bedford: "Interviewed Dec. 2nd by Elizabeth Pidgeon. Pleasant man. Says he has been personally for suffrage for years but wants to represent constituents. Going to call for expressions of suffrage opinion thru the press. Much interested in enrollments, especially men's names. Assured him interview would be confidential." The notes continue: "M.E.P. lists 'probable.'" During the 1920 assembly session, Pidgeon interviewed Gordon and recorded him as saying, "I expect I'll have to vote against it. My wife is against it and I couldn't go against my boss."

The card for Walter H. Robertson, a new Republican delegate from Bristol, also contains several notations: "Considers suffrage a natural right. That amendment is to remove prohibition against a right she already has,"

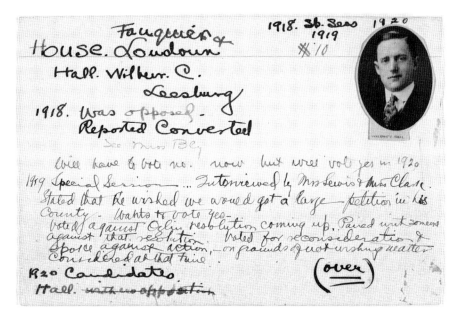

The Equal Suffrage League created index cards for members of the House of Delegates to track their actions and statements on the proposed amendment. *Library of Virginia.*

one of the boldest recorded affirmations of the natural right of women to vote by any Virginia public official. "Thinks Virginia will make mistake not to ratify. Believes sentiment in his section among both sexes is against it. Does not feel prest. He has made up his mind what he will do." Pidgeon's list indicated he was "Favorably doubtful." Another noted, "Reported probably for."

Some legislators proposed in 1919 and early in 1920 to submit to the voters the question of whether to grant Virginia women the vote. Wilbur C. Hall, a few days after winning reelection in Loudoun County, was one of the legislators who appeared to be turning from his former opposition to acceptance of woman suffrage, but he regarded an amendment to the state constitution as preferable to an amendment to the federal constitution. "It's bound to come," he told his interviewer; "Still it would take courage to say no if they suggested a referendum....To the question 'who would vote on that referendum?' he said 'The qualified voters, or course' (looking sheepish.)" Suffragists opposed a referendum, especially if only men were to be allowed to vote in it.

Richard L. Brewer, before he was elected Speaker of the House of Delegates in January, met with Adèle Clark on December 2, 1919, to plan strategy for the attempt to ratify the Nineteenth Amendment. "Advises introduction of resolution in one house preferable senate," the card's notes on the interview record. Though Brewer was doubtful that the assembly would ratify it, "He thinks strength there, passing Senate in time more chance in House." Brewer also suggested introducing an amendment to the state constitution in the House of Delegates. "Urged strongly state amendment. Was told it is too late. Interview satisfactory." The cards could have suggested to Equal Suffrage League lobbyists that their original objective of an amendment to the state constitution might be within reach, but the league had long been committed to the federal amendment, and Clark told Brewer "it was too late" for a state amendment.

ONE DEFEAT AND TWO VICTORIES

Officers and members of the Equal Suffrage League and the National Woman's Party descended on the General Assembly when it convened on January 14, 1920. On January 21, Carrie Chapman Catt, president of the National American Woman Suffrage Association, addressed the House of Delegates with some members of the Senate present. On that day, anti-suffrage activists made one last major attempt to defeat ratification of the Nineteenth Amendment with the issue of race. Before the House session began, they placed on the desk of every delegate a copy of a leaflet that featured photographs of Catt, former NAWSA president Anna Howard Shaw and "'Mrs. R. Jerome Jeffrey' (negro)," and a large body of text that appeared to prove that the suffragists were apostles of racial equality and that Catt had enjoyed Jeffrey's hospitality in her home—had accepted Jeffrey as an equal.[18]

The *Evening Journal* reported that during Catt's speech to the legislators she "denounced as a 'malicious lie' the report that she was 'a guest in the home of a negro.' This and other like reports, she said, were spread to prejudice southerners against the equal suffrage cause." Catt predicted that voters in the future would be more intelligent "than the average man of today" and "prophesied an era when intelligence will be a prerequisite to qualifying for the ballot." Perhaps Catt interjected that comment into her speech in hope of reassuring men who opposed woman suffrage and African American suffrage that the existing difficult registration process would continue to restrict the vote to educated and respectable people. Catt concluded, "Men

THE "THREE IMMEDIATE WOMEN FRIENDS" OF THE ANTHONY FAMILY. SEE BIOGRAPHY OF SUSAN B. ANTHONY, PAGE 1435, BY MRS. IDA HUSTED HARPER.

CARRIE CHAPMAN CATT   The Rev. ANNA HOWARD SHAW   "Mrs. R. JEROME JEFFREY"
(NEGRO)

From Left to Right: Carrie Chapman Catt; The Rev. Anna Howard Shaw; Mrs. R. Jerome Jeffery, Negro woman of Rochester, N. Y. Often "Guest in Anthony Home" with Mrs. Shaw and Mrs. Carrie Chapman Catt, President of National Woman Suffrage Association, to which all Southern Suffragettes belong.

Anti-suffragists placed copies of this leaflet on every desk in the House of Delegates before Carrie Chapman Catt spoke to the General Assembly on January 21, 1920. *Library of Virginia.*

of Virginia, I entreat you to be just to the women." The newspaper reported, "The speaker was frequently applauded."[19]

Members of the General Assembly decided against submitting a referendum to the voters and, as anticipated, refused to ratify the amendment. On February 6, 1920, the Senate rejected the amendment by a vote of 24 to 10, and on February 12, the House of Delegates rejected it 62 to 22. During debate in the Senate, though, according to one newspaper report, several senators who opposed ratification of the Nineteenth Amendment "stated that they would favor submission of an amendment to the State Constitution granting suffrage to women, but that they were unalterably opposed to any amendment to the Federal Constitution which violated the principles of States' rights," by which they meant the right of states to maintain almost impossibly high barriers to African American voting. No doubt some Democratic legislators also feared that if women won the vote in spite of them some of those women might vote for Republicans, whose state and national parties had endorsed woman suffrage in 1916; and no doubt some others decided to change their minds after President Woodrow Wilson publicly urged the General Assembly to ratify the Nineteenth Amendment.[20]

Even though a majority of legislators voted against the Nineteenth Amendment, they could see the handwriting on the wall and voted to change state law to provide that if the Nineteenth Amendment were ratified before the 1920 election, women could vote then if they paid the required $1.50 poll tax and registered as new voters. The "machinery bill," as Equal Suffrage League officials called it, passed the Senate by a vote of 30 to 6 on March 4, and the House of Delegates by a vote of 64 to 17 on March 12. Governor Westmoreland Davis signed it on March 20.[21]

The decade-long campaign and endorsement from thirty-two thousand Virginians persuaded or in effect forced a majority of the legislators to accept woman suffrage, some of them no doubt reluctantly. The General Assembly proposed an amendment to the state constitution to grant Virginia's women the right to vote. Senator Junius E. West introduced and the Senate passed a joint resolution on February 20, by a vote of 28 to 11, and the House passed it on March 12, by a vote of 67 to 10. Along with several minor changes to suffrage provisions in the state constitution, the proposed amendment replaced the phrase "Every male citizen of the United States" in Article II Sections 18 and 20 with "Every citizen of the United States, male or female." The General Assembly would have to pass the amendment again in 1922 before it could be submitted to the voters for ratification or rejection.[22]

Virginia suffragists had succeeded and achieved their original objective of persuading the General Assembly to propose a woman suffrage amendment to the state constitution. Because of the long amendment process, it turned out to be too late to make a difference. Largely absent from the published histories of the suffrage movement and poorly reported in the state's newspapers, the votes by large majorities in both houses on the proposed state constitutional amendment attracted surprisingly little attention and comment, even in the surviving correspondence of the state's suffragists.

Senator Harry Flood Byrd, who had opposed woman suffrage since he was first elected in 1915, voted against ratification of the Nineteenth Amendment, but he voted for the law to permit women to vote in 1920 and for the proposed amendment to the state constitution. Among the senators who supported woman suffrage, E. Lee Trinkle of Wytheville was elected governor in 1921; Junius West was elected lieutenant governor in

1921 and 1925; and G. Walter Mapp, who had supported woman suffrage and planned legislative strategy with Valentine and other league leaders, had strong support from his old suffragist allies when he unsuccessfully ran against Byrd for the Democratic Party nomination for governor in 1925. At that time, Nora Houston informed Adèle Clark that at Byrd's order one of his supporters removed from the Virginia State Library a copy of a 1918 edition of the *Winchester Evening Star* (which Byrd owned) in which he had opposed votes for women. The story has not been, and probably cannot be, proved or disproved, but Clark's papers preserve an undated typed press release from the "Custodial Committee of the Records of the Equal Suffrage League of Virginia" (Adèle Clark, Jessie Townsend, Mary Pollard Clarke, Marie Leahey and Faith W. Morgan). Pasted to it is a racist anti-suffrage editorial clipped from the March 9, 1918 issue of the *Evening Star*. Its wording, however, does not resemble Byrd's usual speaking style.[23]

A writer for the *Norfolk Ledger-Dispatch* composed one of the few newspaper commentaries on the proposed state amendment but, like most other observers, conflated the work of the Equal Suffrage League and the National Woman's Party and also confused the General Assembly's votes on the Nineteenth Amendment, the law to allow women to register and vote in 1920, and the resolution to amend the state constitution. In one critical particular, however, the writer got it exactly right: "No cause before the Virginia legislature ever was backed by a more determined and aggressive lobby than was furnished by the women favoring the Federal amendment. The anti-suffragists were equally determined, but they were far less numerous."[24]

RATIFICATION OF THE NINETEENTH AMENDMENT

The Tennessee legislature ratified the Nineteenth Amendment on August 18, 1920. That was the last of the thirty-six legislative acts required to make it part of the Constitution of the United States. Surprisingly, few Virginia suffragists commented on the ratification in print or in their private correspondence. Edith Clark Cowles described a few weeks later the moment when she learned about ratification of the Nineteenth Amendment. "At last, when victory really came," she recalled, "some of us were so stunned we could hardly realize that we had over night become people and would count in the general run of matters."[25]

A DAY OF TRIUMPH AND DIGNITY

VIRGINIA WOMEN VOTE

In October 1919, long before ratification of the Nineteenth Amendment was assured, Lila Meade Valentine promoted the organization of citizenship conferences throughout Virginia to be conducted under the auspices of the extension division of the University of Virginia to prepare women to register and vote. Valentine and officials at the University of Virginia agreed to hire Mary Elizabeth Pidgeon, based on her speaking ability and successful work enrolling suffrage supporters, to be state director. Pidgeon began the work with a three-day School of Citizenship at the university on April 22, 23 and 24, 1920. She took the program on the road and conducted sessions in several Virginia towns and cities prior to the election in November.

In that election, the state's women had to be prepared not only to elect a president, a vice president, a United States senator, members of the House of Representatives, and some local officers but also to vote on six proposals to amend the state constitution: to change qualifications for some city and county officials; to authorize modifications in forms of local government; to allow women to serve on local school boards; to change the procedures for levying taxes for public schools; to make school attendance mandatory for school-age children; and to authorize referenda to permit the state to issue bonds to raise money for road construction.

REGISTERING TO VOTE

Virginia's constitution and election laws required men to pay the necessary poll tax six months before an election, that they register during a thirty-day period and that registration cease thirty days before an election. Ratification of the Nineteenth Amendment effectively excised the limiting word *male* from the state constitution's description of who could register and vote. The March 1920 state law suffragists referred to as the "machinery bill" set no time limit for women to pay the required poll tax and register after ratification of the amendment. Therefore, Virginia women were able to pay the $1.50 poll tax as new voters and register between September 2 and October 2, 1920.[1]

Ida Mae Thompson wrote enthusiastically on August 24, less than a week after ratification of the amendment, "The 'Machine' here in Richmond has informed us that it is ready to register our women at once…and we hope that the powers that be in other parts of the State will be equally as helpful." Some registrars resigned, however, rather than register women. Frank L. Dunn resigned as registrar at Trevilians in Louisa County and reportedly "expressed his heartfelt disgust at the action of the Tennessee legislature" that provided the last ratification necessary to place the Nineteenth Amendment in the Constitution. Faith Morgan's sister Fanny Walcott reported from Hampton that the city registrar had resigned rather than enroll women voters. When Hermine Moore attempted to register in Chesterfield County, the registrar groused, "I don't know nothing about you ladies voting and can't let you register." Charlottesville resident Elizabeth W. Lewis complained that although she had paid her poll tax at the treasurer's office, "there is no registrar in my precinct." Anne Harris and her sister went to the courthouse in Henrico County to register, but "to our chagrin and disappointment, we were told that we could not register except on Wednesdays and Saturdays from nine to two." On the other hand, Eugenia Jobson and Sarah Wormeley served as assistant registrars of voters in the city of Richmond. Tradition records that Lila Meade Valentine was too unwell to leave home to register but that somebody persuaded a registrar to go to her home and register her there. She registered on September 27, 1920.[2]

Registering to vote for the first time was exciting. In some places, women even began to register immediately after the proclamation of ratification. In Winchester, Isabelle E. Baker and Frances W. Beverley registered to vote on August 27, and a few others registered before the formal September 2 opening of registration. At a meeting to encourage registration in Newport

Both Democratic and Republican women urged party members to register. *The Valentine*.

News, "Two old ladies" ages eighty and eighty-four eagerly attended, and one of the first women to register there announced her desire to become mayor. Fanny Walcott reported that she and another unmarried woman, both evidently heads of their own households, "had considerable fun with the registrar." When asked their jobs, they called themselves housewives, even though they were unmarried. The registrar identified each of them as married. Walcott objected, "& he said how can you be housewifes if you are not married?"[3]

In many places, the number of women who registered exceeded expectations. The registrar in Norton in the southwestern county of Wise prepared to register more than seven hundred women, but only a week into the process he was convinced that many more women than that would register. That was fairly typical of the scattered reports during the registration period. Nannie Kent Ellis of Montgomery County recalled with pleasure in 1936 that in spite of little support for woman suffrage in the county before 1920, "I do not think our efforts were entirely lost, for after Woman Suffrage was won, and women registered for the first election, 42 women registered at the Shawsville precinct. The number of men voters on the registration books at that time being about 80, we regarded that 42 women as rather good…but a number of the older women have not voted since Prohibition ceased to be an issue."[4]

The social convention of not stating the ages of adult women hindered some of them in registering. The state constitution required that the date of birth be entered on the registration form, but Rosalie B. Kelsey of Bedford County refused to give her birthdate or age to the registrar. Kelsey acknowledged to the registrar only "that she was more than 21 years of age." The registrar could see that. "As a matter of fact," he noted, "she is supposed to be about 75." (A few months earlier, Kelsey had informed the census enumerator that she was born in 1854 and was therefore about sixty-six.) The registrar requested an official opinion from Attorney General John R. Saunders about what he should do about a woman who was clearly old enough but would not state her birthdate. The attorney general, whose wife had been a member of the Equal Suffrage League of Saluda, in Middlesex County, informed the registrar that "the mere statement that the person making application to register is considerably over twenty-one years of age, accompanied by the physical appearance of being over that age, is not a sufficient compliance with the provisions of the Constitution." He advised the registrar to give Kelsey one more chance to provide the date and comply.[5]

The state's constitution and laws required applicants to give correct answers to any questions the registrar asked about the person's qualifications to register. Democratic registrars regularly and without any specific legal authority stretched the wording in Article II, Section 20, of the state constitution and in Chapter 8, Section 73, of the Code of Virginia that required correct answers under oath to "any and all questions" about a person's qualifications to permit other questions as if those other questions established an applicant's legal capability to register. They asked Republicans and African Americans questions on a wide variety of subjects and disqualified people who gave what they ruled were unsatisfactory answers. A few years later, a prominent Republican lawyer published a list of questions he charged that a registrar had posed to "the wife of one of the most intelligent men in this State," who was almost certainly a Republican. Among the questions were:

> "How many historical flags has the United States?"
>
> "Who discovered the Rocky Mountains and when?"
>
> "Name the first state to grant suffrage to women and when."
>
> "What State passed the Port bill and when?"
>
> "What State had its boundary changed three times by the U.S. Government and what was its number when admitted?"
>
> "What State was the last to ratify the woman suffrage amendment?"
>
> "How many men between 18 and 45 years of age served in the World War from the United States?"
>
> "What State was originally named Albemarle?"[6]

Ada Alexander told Chloe Bly, a member of the Equal Suffrage League of Leesburg, about the frustrating time she had when she tried to get women to register. "Less than 45 women have registered to date," Alexander complained. "They give silly reasons like, 'don't want to tell any man my age', 'am afraid they'll ask some questions I can't answer about the Constitution', 'I didn't know when the time-limit was.'" The "funny thing about it," Bly observed, "is that the men who have opposed us for years, and who now want public office, are the ones who quite brazenly urge upon us the duty of getting the women registered!" Those practical political men readily accepted woman suffrage, which many of them had long opposed, after it was in their interest to do so. The following summer, when candidates for statewide office, the General Assembly and local offices were mounting their campaigns, Ida Mae Thompson remarked with amused satisfaction, "We (the women) are the most popular people ever. The candidates all <u>think</u> they have always wanted the women to have the vote and have always worked hard to attain this end."[7]

IMPEDIMENTS TO AFRICAN AMERICAN REGISTRATION

The eagerness with which African American women paid the poll tax and sought to register clearly demonstrated how important they and their families believed the franchise to be. The right to vote was an essential element of citizenship, and all but the very youngest of them could remember when the Virginia Constitutional Convention of 1901–2 deprived most African American men of that right. Although the women did not openly organize and campaign for the right to vote, they were every bit as committed to voting as the most active white suffragists. The day before registration opened in Richmond, a newspaper reported, "Colored churches and social organizations are urging the women to qualify as voters at the first opportunity."[8]

Maggie Lena Walker and Ora Brown Stokes planned a massive voter registration project for African American women in Richmond. Had white fear of African American voting not been so strong and widespread as it was, they would certainly have been in the spotlight with Lila Meade Valentine, Sophie Meredith, Elizabeth Lewis, Pauline Adams and the other advocates of woman suffrage all along.

Walker was the most famous African American woman in Virginia and enjoyed national celebrity as a successful business executive and civic leader. For almost forty years, she had been an officer in the Independent Order of St. Luke, a mutual benefit society. In fact, she was secretary of her chapter by the time she graduated from high school. In 1890, Walker became the order's Right Worthy Grand Chief. She organized events, attended conferences and began a juvenile department for the community's children. Nine years later, when the order was facing severe financial and membership problems, Walker won election to its highest office, Right Worthy Grand Secretary. Under her leadership, the order founded a newspaper and a department

Left: Maggie Lena Walker, of Richmond, was the most successful and well-known of all African American business and civic leaders in Virginia. *Library of Virginia*.

Right: Ora Brown Stokes was an influential and well-known leader among African American women in Richmond and throughout Virginia. *From A. B. Caldwell*, History of the American Negro: Virginia Edition *(Caldwell Publishing, 1921)*.

store. In 1903, it opened St. Luke Penny Savings Bank. Walker was president of the bank from its founding until 1930—the first African American woman bank president in the United States. Her bank later merged with two other African American banks in Richmond and became the Consolidated Bank and Trust. Walker's advocacy of education and of the interests of women and children together with her natural abilities as a leader and inspiring speaker earned her a nationwide following. Walker noted in her diary that on September 11, 1920, she paid her first poll tax in order to register to vote, and she registered three days later.[9]

Stokes graduated from Virginia Normal and Collegiate Institute (later Virginia State University) at age sixteen and studied at the Chicago School of Civics and Philanthropy. In Richmond, she was active in support of missionary work in her church, ran a millinery store and, beginning about 1911, engaged in a variety of social reform activities. Stokes founded the National Protective League for Negro Girls in 1916. During World War I, Stokes was chair of the Colored Women's Section of the Council of

National Defense and regimental mother to African American soldiers stationed at Camp Lee, near Petersburg. In 1918, she became the first female African American probation officer in Richmond working with juveniles. Stokes also was the first woman to serve as a vice president of the National Race Congress, and she often attended conventions of the Virginia State Federation of Colored Women's Clubs and the National Association of Colored Women. She was well-enough known and respected to be one of the very few women to have her own separate entry in the 630-page 1921 biographical reference work *History of the American Negro, Virginia Edition.*[10]

Walker and Stokes organized such a successful registration drive that they had to demand that the city assign more registrars to African American neighborhoods to reduce the waiting time. Newspapers reported that Mary E. Sparrow, Puralee Sampson, Blanch Wines, nurse Katie D. Pratt and schoolteacher Rosa DeWitt were among the first to pay their poll taxes and register to vote. Adèle Clark and several other white women personally went into African American neighborhoods to make certain that black women who wanted to register were not victims of intimidation or discrimination at the hands of white male registrars. Clark and the others were exceptions to the rule; unlike a majority of other white women, they believed that all women should be able to register and vote, not merely white women.

Elsewhere, African American women organized registration drives. In Phoebus and Hampton, African American men helped women train for anticipated hostile encounters with white registrars and drilled them in detail about the state constitution. It was a proud day for the women who succeeded. Nine faculty members of Virginia Normal and Industrial Institute (later Virginia State University) in Ettrick, near Petersburg, posed for a joint photograph on the occasion. Members of the Colored Women's Republican Club of Roanoke helped register voters in that city. Millie B. Paxton, the club's president, had attended Hampton Normal and Agricultural Institute (later Hampton University) and the Virginia Seminary, in Lynchburg. After her marriage in 1895, she lived in Roanoke, and she later worked as the attendance officer in the city's racially segregated schools. Paxton led a women's Bible class for many years at First Baptist Church and was vice president of the missionary society. She served on the board of the Lott Carey Baptist Foreign Mission Convention. Paxton was a member or leader of nearly every African American woman's organization in Roanoke, the founding president of the Colored Women's Republican Club of Roanoke and an officer in the Virginia State Federation of Colored Women's Clubs.[11]

Nine faculty members at Virginia Normal and Industrial Institute posed for this photograph on the day they registered to vote. *Virginia State University.*

African American women faced obstacles in many places, obstacles even more formidable than other women faced, even white Republican women. Newspaper reports of registration often gave separate numbers for white and African American women with the apparent objective of encouraging more white women to register to counter the new African American voters. A Berryville newspaper recorded the registration of three African American women during the third week of September and published their names along with the names of a "large number of white women" who during the same period "joined the ranks of voters." Fanny Walcott reported six days into the registration process that 122 women had registered in Newport News "of whom 36 were colored." One of the local newspapers, she continued, "said it was the women of better families (both White & Colored) who were registering." The headlines on a Richmond *News Leader* story read, "One Time This Morning Negro Women Were in Possession," indicating that they filled the registrar's office,

"With White Women Standing Outside in Corridor." Black women who took or seized precedence over white women fulfilled the fears of many opponents of woman suffrage. The *Richmond Planet* reported the following week that registrars then required African American women to register in the basement of city hall.[12]

Following a repetition of that episode, Mary Mason Anderson Williams, president of the Virginia Association Opposed to Woman Suffrage, issued a statement that almost bristled with fear that African American women who voted threatened white supremacy. "In view of the fact that colored women are registering in large numbers, evidently with the purpose of creating a balance of power, which may cause race problems and disturb present good conditions," Williams advised "the women of Virginia who have consistently opposed woman suffrage, and who still oppose it, as wrong in principle and contrary to the best interests of women and the State…to register and to be prepared to exercise their influence for the best interests of all our people, both white and colored, and to oppose any radical or dangerous changes which may be proposed by agitators flushed with undue self-importance and actuated by a desire for political prominence and office." Williams registered on January 24, 1921, long after the election.[13]

Impediments to black registration are best documented in the Hampton Roads area because in October 1920 the National Association for the Advancement of Colored People sent field agent Addie W. Hunton to Hampton to investigate and report on "the recent non-registration of colored women" there. In spite of the promise of some registrars in the area to assist women, Hunton collected testimony from women in Hampton and neighboring Phoebus who told her that they had to return to the registrar's office several times before they were able to register and that some women finally just gave up. Registrars sometimes gave white women priority or protracted the procedure for African Americans so much that several white women registered before even one African American could complete the process. They sometimes gave African American women blank sheets of paper on which to register but gave white women forms that indicated the information to be recorded. In order to know whose applications to speed through and whose to obstruct, the registrar asked light-skinned women their husbands' names; because registrars may have known who their husbands were, registrars could easily ascertain the legal race of African American women.[14]

The women found it humiliating, especially when registrars asked irrelevant questions and then refused to register them because they did not give satisfactory answers. Sarah Haws Baker Fields survived the ordeal in Hampton. Among the questions the registrar asked Fields and that she correctly answered on her second attempt were:

"How is Supt. of public instruction elected?"

"How are vacancies filled and what is his term of office?"

"What is the maximum and minimum number of section districts in the State of Virginia?"

"What are the exceptions of compulsion"—Hunton's typing error for *compulsory*—"education?"

"Who are exempted from paying poll tax and yet eligible to vote?"

Fields's husband was the well-known African American attorney George Washington Fields, and her daughter was Inez Catherine Fields, who became one of the first African American women to practice law in Virginia. He assisted some of the women to register and gave Hunton assistance in her investigation, too. One woman went to the local circuit court judge after twice being refused registration in Hampton and finally succeeded in registering. Another reported that in Hampton "colored women were so insulted when they attempted to register, that one woman said, 'I could kill the clerk who questioned me; I could kill his wife and children.'"[15]

In Norfolk, Hunton learned, the situation had been even worse. The registrar there ruled that Emma Virginia Lee Kelley and four other women failed to answer correctly the questions he asked them and refused to register them. They engaged several African American lawyers and took the registrar to court, where he humiliated himself when he gave an incorrect answer to at least one of the same questions he had asked them and disqualified them for answering incorrectly:

"When may the writ of habeas corpus be suspended?"

"In what year was the Constitution of the United States adopted?"

"How long can the House of Representatives take recess without the consent of the Senate?"

"Into what named divisions are the functions of the United States government divided by the United States?"[16]

Challenging the eligibility of such a prominent woman as Kelley may have been a deliberate strategy to discourage lesser-known or less-bold women from making the attempt to register. Kelley was one of the best-known African American women in southeastern Virginia. A longtime superintendent of the Sunday school in one of Norfolk's largest Baptist churches and active in support of its missionary work, she also was a founder of the Daughters of the Improved Benevolent and Protective Order of Elks of the World and credited with establishing many of its temples in the United States. Like Ora Brown Stokes, of Richmond, "Mother Kelley," as she became known, rated her own separate biography in the 1921 *History of the American Negro, Virginia Edition*. Her entry concluded, "She believes that better conditions are to be hoped for by improvement in the schools, by better housing and by woman suffrage."[17]

EMMA V. KELLEY

Emma V. Kelley took the voter registrar to court after he refused to register her in Norfolk. *From A.B. Caldwell,* History of the American Negro: Virginia Edition *(Caldwell Publishing, 1921).*

Editor John Mitchell Jr. of the *Richmond Planet* remarked on the difficulties African American women had encountered when they went to register and predicted that their problems were not over. "Some women are getting tired trying to get ready for voting," he began, "and they will get more tired, when they attempt to exercise that right at the polls. They have though what their male friends do not possess. They have the full power of speech and they know how to use it." At that time anywhere in the southern states it was literally dangerous for a black man to challenge or question a white man for any reason. "The tongue is a powerful weapon in the mouth of a woman," Mitchell concluded, "and the men, even the democratic men know it."[18]

Early in 1921, the NAACP convened a small conference in Washington of women from several states to lobby Alice Paul of the National Woman's Party for assistance in securing the vote for African American women, but Paul was not helpful. Ora Brown Stokes and Lizzie L. Stanard from Richmond attended, as did Mary E. Henderson from Falls Church. Maggie Walker did not attend but promised officials of the NAACP, "I will gladly join in with the women to protect the 'Susan B. Anthony Amendment' which the women of this Country, fought so hard to have passed." Walker and the other African American women had not been able to work openly for woman suffrage, but they claimed full ownership of the right along with the white women who had.[19]

REGISTRATION COMPLETED

The registrar in the city of Richmond published a detailed report of the numbers of white and black men and women who registered in each of the city's voting precincts, 10,645 white women and 2,410 black women. In Roanoke, about 4,500 women registered; reports on African American registration there varied from about 500 to 655. The registrar in Lynchburg reported that 1,312 white women registered in the city along with 330 black women, and the registrar in Wythe County reported the day before registration concluded that about 1,200 women had registered there. The state published no figures indicating how many women registered and may not have even compiled that data. The approximate number can be estimated by comparing the 1916 and 1920 presidential election returns. In the 1916 election, 153,984 Virginians voted, and in the 1920 election, 231,000 voted, an increase of 77,016, almost exactly 50 percent—a large increase but still a small percentage of the whole number of adults (only about 18.5 percent), but since adoption of the Virginia Constitution of 1902, a large majority of both black and white Virginia men were effectively disfranchised.[20]

New women voters probably accounted for a large part of the increase. The Democratic vote increased about 37.8 percent, but the Republican vote increased by about 77 percent. The larger proportional increase for Republicans may reflect the willingness of leading Republican men (and perhaps members of their families as well) to embrace woman suffrage before many leading Democratic men did. Moreover, it is very probable that most or all the African American women who registered voted for Republicans. That diminished the Democrats' majority in the state only marginally, from about 66.8 percent to about 61.3 percent.

ELECTION DAY

Virginia voters had to select from three presidential candidates: Republican Warren G. Harding, Democrat James M. Cox and Socialist Eugene V. Debs. They also had to elect a United States senator, a congressman from each of ten districts and local officials in some communities. They also had to vote for or against the six proposed amendments to the state constitution. Election Day, November 2, 1920, was cloudy and cool in much of Virginia. Photographs published in some of the state's newspapers show women wearing long coats as they stood in line waiting to vote. In Winchester, "Election officials had difficulty in handling the long lines of men and women voters, some of the latter coming in the rain with nursing babies in their arms. Much time was lost showing women how to mark ballots."[21]

Blanche Winder may have been the first woman to vote in Norfolk, certainly the first in her precinct. She and her husband arrived early, at the same time poll workers began setting up for the day. Winder posed for the photographer of the *Norfolk Ledger-Dispatch*, and the newspaper published

On Election Day in 1920, women and men lined up to vote in every precinct in the state, as at this Richmond voting place. *The Valentine.*

the photograph on the front page of that afternoon's paper. Typical for the time, it identified her by her husband's initials as Mrs. W.J. Winder. The paper printed two photographs of women waiting in line under the headline "Voting Lines Plentifully Besprinkled with Women." The following day, the paper published three more photographs of women at the city's polling places. Male reporters everywhere regarded voting women as a true novelty. Almost none of them, though, thought it important to ask the women what they thought about casting their first votes or reported what the big day meant to them.[22]

The morning newspaper in Norfolk, the *Virginian-Pilot and Norfolk Landmark*, published two photographs of women, some of them knitting, in lines at polling places under the faux humorous headline, "'Women First' Went into Discard When Voterettes Lined Up with the Voters." It also reported a conversation that took place while women were waiting to vote:

"This is the proudest day of my life!" one excited woman exclaimed.

A nearby newlywed woman responded, "The proudest day? Why, have you forgotten your wedding day?"

To which the first woman replied, "No, but the Lord gave me the graces that won for me a wedding day, but it took more than God-given graces to bring about this day!" She was proud that they had worked for and won the right to vote. The newspaper also reported that some women mistakenly deposited sample ballots in the ballot box "and took the real ballots home as souvenirs."[23]

A headline in the *Roanoke Times* announced, "Roanoke Women Voted Yesterday as If They Had Voted for Years." The report began, "Roanoke women came to the front in politics yesterday and made their appearance felt in every precinct in the city. From early morning until the closing of the polls, old women and those girls just over the age line made their appearance at the polls. They came on the helping arm of grey haired husbands, on the nimble and muscular arm of the gentlemen friends, some carrying babies, others carrying chairs or stools and arrived in everything from the jitney to the highest priced limo[u]sines." A later newspaper reported, "A number of business houses and department stores gave their women employees the privilege of reporting late so that they would have every opportunity to cast their ballot and do it early in the day. As result it was notable that voting lines at the polls were divided about fifty-fifty as between men and women." In fact, official reports indicate that more than 50 percent of the voters in Roanoke that day were women. The *Richmond Planet*, an African American newspaper, concluded its report on voting in

Roanoke with praise for the work of the president and members of the city's Colored Women's Republican Club. "Everybody seemed in the best of humor and long will be remembered that long line of old and young colored women on November 2 in Roanoke."[24]

"Mrs. Mary Donahoe," the *Richmond Times-Dispatch* reported, "seventy-one years old, of Laurel Street, has the distinction of being the first voter to cast a ballot in the Third Precinct, Clay Ward. She arrived at the voting place long before the polls opened." The paper noted with approval that she "voted the straight Democratic ticket." Adèle Clark and Nora Houston also arrived at their polling place in Richmond early, at 5:30 a.m., to vote and begin the daylong campaign to monitor the voting and assist Democratic Party workers. Clark, Sarah Wormeley and Marie Leahey borrowed Lila Meade Valentine's automobile to make "a tour of the polling places, working like veteran ward workers" for the Democratic ticket.[25]

A large number of women, both white and black, who lived in the Highland Park neighborhood of Richmond, discovered when they went to vote that their names were not on the poll books. About seventy-five of them "besieged the office" of the city registrar "clamoring to know why after registering they had been left out of the registration books." A judge ruled that those women should show their poll tax receipts to the registrar, obtain a certificate of registration and then return to the polling place to vote. In another part of the city, some voters' names appeared in the wrong poll book.[26]

Reports from smaller cities tended to be shorter, and only a few reports of voting in rural areas survive. A Martinsville woman gave her husband marching orders first thing in the morning. "Put on your collar and your coat," she instructed him. "This is a day of triumph and dignity." In Danville, "The women were among the first to go to the polls" that morning. "For some it was the earliest duty of the day taking precedence even of household duties." Moreover, "For the first time in a quarter of a century negro workers appeared at the polls" in Danville "and were assisted by white republicans who openly instructed negroes how to mark their tickets. They appeared jubilant at the early movement of the colored vote. This fact had the effect of spurring to action white men and women who had previously showed no great interest in the campaign and lethargy had been abandoned by noon and at every voting precinct men and women were waiting to cast their votes."[27]

"Election day passed off very quietly," the newspaper in the Shenandoah County town of Woodstock reported in a fairly typical manner, "the ladies receiving the usual courtesies due their sex." The two newspapers in Fredericksburg reported in identical language, "The women took to voting just as a duck takes to water and looked like old veterans." Neither paper mentioned Janetta FitzHugh, who had worked for nearly a decade to gain the franchise for women and was one of the first women in the city to register. Laura Davenport recalled in 1936 that in the West Virginia border town of Bluefield "there were but few of the women in our little town who did not go to the polls in 1920 to cast first vote." In Hampton, "the line of voters was kept up all day, as the women were out in full to cast their ballots." In neighboring Phoebus, with its large African American population, the Republican presidential candidate carried the town.[28]

Men and women of both races stood in line together to vote. That offended some white people. A Newport News lawyer wrote to the governor the following spring and complained, "It is intensely disagreeable for our wives and daughters to have to stand in a long line of white and colored men and women before they can proceed to vote." He suggested passage of a law to require judges of election to form black and white voters into separate lines and allow voters to cast their ballots from each line alternately. He pointed out that members of both races would be "treated exactly alike"—separate but equal.[29]

Jessie Townsend of Norfolk was one of the few prominent suffragists to leave a record of casting her first vote. Her account is remarkably undramatic and lacks all sense of the personal importance and revolutionary character of the occasion. "Have just returned from voting in my precinct," she began a long handwritten letter to Edith Clark Cowles at 4:30 p.m., "& want to bustle around town now & see what's what." Townsend had planned to vote earlier, "but having no cook & three surveyors to feed"—men who worked for the Townsends' real estate development company—"I could not leave home until now." She criticized the men who supervised the voting at her precinct for allowing campaign workers closer to the polling place than the law allowed, "but everything was quiet & orderly."[30]

As anticipated, Democratic presidential candidate James M. Cox easily won the election in Virginia, but Republican Warren G. Harding won a majority of electoral college votes and was elected president. And Virginia women apparently voted overwhelmingly in favor of ratifying the six amendments to the state constitution.

It must have been a very great disappointment to Lila Meade Valentine that she was not well enough to go out on the damp and threatening day to cast a ballot in the first election in which Virginia women participated.

The Richmond *Evening Dispatch* reported that she was even "too ill to be interviewed" about the momentous event but that she "watched the progress of the day with unabated interest, receiving bulletins throughout the polling hours." Her relative and most trusted collaborator in the decade-long campaign for woman suffrage, Elizabeth Lewis, probably did not vote, either, because she may not have returned to Lynchburg in time from visiting her niece Lady Astor in England.[31]

The author of an editorial in the *Richmond Times-Dispatch* on the day after the election could not refrain from taking a glancing shot at the Nineteenth Amendment. "Whether or not one approves the method by which they were enfranchised," he observed of the women of Richmond, and "whether or not one approves their presence in politics, no one will be so churlish as to deny the patent fact that they have more than made good in this, their first, campaign, and their first opportunity to back up their opinions with their ballots." He continued in a pleasantly surprised tone, "Throughout the entire campaign they have been active, vigilant and tireless. They have comprised in large measure the audience at every party rally. They qualified and registered in unexpected numbers, and for twenty-four hours every day they have been on the job; assisting the registrar, straightening out the inevitable tangles resultant upon so heavy an increase in the electorate, and in arousing dormant enthusiasm."[32]

DISAPPOINTMENTS

Some women discovered during voter registration in 1920 and in the aftermath of the election that politics could be as unsavory as opponents of woman suffrage had often portrayed it. In the Seventh Congressional District in northwestern Virginia, which included the Blue Ridge Mountains and much of the Shenandoah Valley, defeated Republican candidate John Paul challenged the election of Democrat Thomas W. Harrison. Irregularities and outright corruption of several sorts during registration and on Election Day had been unusually bad. The House of Representatives did not rule on Paul's challenge until early in 1922 because before ratification of the Twentieth Amendment in 1933, congressmen elected in even-numbered years did not take their seats until December of the following odd-numbered year. The House of Representatives disallowed a great many votes, both Democratic and Republican, both men's and women's, but more Democratic votes than Republican votes and declared Paul the legally elected congressman. He was the husband of Katherine Seymour Paul, founding president of the Equal Suffrage League of Rockingham County, and as a member of the Senate of Virginia, he had favored ratification of the Nineteenth Amendment. That was the last time that any candidate for Congress from Virginia successfully challenged the election of a competitor. Several years later, Democrat Gertrude Barton, a former member of the Equal Suffrage League of Winchester, angrily recalled, perhaps with some exaggeration, "All of our votes (the women's votes) were thrown out…except mine & mrs. Holmes Conrad's"—Georgia Bryan Forman Conrad, widow of a prominent local attorney. "Of course the women were furious," Barton continued, "especially as it seemed to be only a technical thing," noncompliance with the constitution and laws Democratic men had adopted to limit voting as much as possible to respectable and politically reliable white men.[33]

THE REST OF THEIR LIVES

VIRGINIA WOMEN AND THE VOTE AFTER 1920

With suffrage achieved, the women who had worked for it entered new phases in their lives. Obituaries of suffragists through the 1920s and 1930s usually referred to their work, but women who lived longer sometimes outlived their suffrage fame. For those women, writers of obituaries often did not know about that important part of their lives' work, and by the times of their deaths their suffrage careers had faded from local memory.

Officers of the National Woman's Party in Virginia and of the Equal Suffrage League generally went their separate ways politically. Several National Woman's Party activists joined the movement for a national constitutional amendment to guarantee women equal rights in all respects. The Equal Suffrage League formed itself into the nonpartisan Virginia League of Women Voters in two meetings in the Capitol in the autumn of 1920. And African American women, with their own particular interests to serve after they obtained the right to vote in the racially segregated state, formed a separate but short-lived Negro Women Voters' League of Virginia with Ora Brown Stokes as state president. The Virginia League of Women Voters remained a purely white women's organization for thirty-five or more years.

THE FIRST CANDIDATES FOR OFFICE

Few of the most active suffragists entered elective politics. Elizabeth Otey was the best-known of those who did. She sought and won the Republican Party nomination for superintendent of public instruction in 1921. She was the first woman a political party nominated for statewide office in Virginia. Otey's early scholarship on working people—especially wage-earning women—actually inclined her toward the Socialist Party. In fact, she voted for Socialist Eugene V. Debs for president in 1920, in part because he was imprisoned for his antiwar political speeches during World War I as some suffragists had been imprisoned for their political actions. In the 1930s, Otey ran unsuccessfully for the House of Delegates and the United States Senate as a Socialist. She may have sought office as a Republican in 1921 because of the Virginia Republican Party's endorsement of woman suffrage during the 1910s or following her late father's political affiliation rather than her mother's.

The Republican Party's state convention in 1921 voted to exclude most of the African Americans who had been elected delegates to it. As a result, the lily-white Republican ticket faced opposition from what people called a lily-black Republican ticket. John Mitchell Jr., editor and publisher of the *Richmond Planet*, was the candidate for governor, and Richmond banker and social reformer Maggie Lena Walker opposed Otey and incumbent Democrat Harris Hart for superintendent of public instruction. Otey received more than 59,000 votes out of more than 208,000 cast, less than one-third, which was about typical for Republican candidates at that time. Otey received the largest percentages of votes in traditional Republican regions in the mountains and valleys of western Virginia. Walker received fewer than 7,000 votes, 1,635 of them in Richmond and much of the remainder in areas with large African American populations.[1]

Several lesser-known women ran for office in 1921. Lillie Davis Custis of Accomack County, a self-described independent socialist, ran for governor that year but received few votes. National Woman's Party officer Mary Lockwood ran for the House of Delegates as a Republican in 1921 but lost. At least seven other women also ran for the House of Delegates that year. Three other Republicans lost in the general election: Nannie Kate Reynolds of Pittsylvania County, Ann Atkinson Chamberlayne of Charlotte County and Josephine Dickenson Buck of Russell County. Janet Stuart Oldershaw Durham and Mary Perkins Bell, both former members of the Equal Suffrage League, ran for but failed to win the nomination of the Democratic Party in

SARAH LEE FAIN

HELEN T. HENDERSON

SALLIE C. BOOKER

CALDWELL V.

HENDERSON H. R.

Emma Lee S. White

Between 1923 and 1929, six women won election to the House of Delegates. *Library of Virginia*.

the city of Richmond, and Eugénie Yancey, former president of the Equal Suffrage League of Bedford, unsuccessfully sought the party's nomination in Bedford County. Maude E. Mundin, also of Richmond, was the only female candidate for the House of Delegates on the lily-black Republican ticket. It is entirely possible that some other women may have sought nomination in 1921 but lost in party conventions or primaries.

During the remainder of the 1920s, no women ran for the state Senate, but during the decade six won election to the House of Delegates. Sarah Lee Fain of Norfolk won election in 1923 to the first of three consecutive two-year terms. Helen T. Henderson also won election to the House in 1923 to represent the counties of Buchanan and Russell. She died after being nominated for a second term in 1925. Her daughter, Helen Ruth Henderson, was elected to one term in 1927. Sallie Cook Booker, a Martinsville schoolteacher, won the first of two consecutive elections in 1925, and Nancy Melvina "Vinnie" Caldwell, of Galax, also a teacher, was elected to one term in 1927. Caldwell was the only one of the six who had taken part in the campaign for the vote; she had been a member of the Equal Suffrage League in neighboring Grayson County, but the very few surviving records do not disclose whether she had been notably active. Six women ran for the House of Delegates in 1929. Emma Lee Smith White of Gloucester County was the only victor. She served two consecutive two-year terms and was the last woman to serve in the General Assembly until 1954. No woman won election to the Virginia Senate until 1977.[2]

During the first decade that Virginia women voted, they had some notable successes in changing Virginia laws for the benefit of women, children and working people. The League of Women Voters persuaded the governor to establish a Children's Code Commission in 1921. The four women (including suffragists Nora Houston of Richmond and Fannie King of Staunton) and five men on the commission proposed twenty-six bills at the 1922 session of the General Assembly, including measures for pensions for mothers, a compulsory school attendance law (which the constitutional amendment ratified in 1920 authorized), establishment of a new state welfare board and regulation of child labor. The General Assembly passed those and other measures, such as requiring fire escapes in public schools, creating a children's bureau within the state department of health, requiring some public hospitals and institutions to offer occupational training, creating the first of what ultimately became a statewide system of juvenile and domestic relations courts, and appropriating matching funds for the federal Sheppard-Towner Act to provide prenatal and child care for rural women. In 1923, league officials created the awkwardly named but influential Virginia Women's Council of Legislative Chairmen of State Organizations to coordinate lobbying at the General Assembly.

THE REST OF THEIR LIVES

The most famous Virginia suffragist, Lila Meade Valentine, never regained her health after an influenza attack early in 1920 and resigned as president of the Equal Suffrage League in a letter to its September 20, 1920 final meeting. After a decade of hard work and personal sacrifice as the foremost Virginia champion of votes for women, Valentine, sadly, never voted. The founders of the Virginia League of Women Voters honored her and her work for woman suffrage by electing her honorary state chair. Valentine died early in the morning of July 14, 1921, in a Richmond hospital following abdominal surgery. Carrie Chapman Catt reflected that Valentine's "was the type of character which has builded our Republic and ever carried forward the flag of progress….Even from her sick bed she led on. Brave, beautiful intrepid soul! What a loss she is, only those of us know, who have heard her public speeches, shared her private counsel and realized through long association, the never surrender quality of her character. She will remain enshrined in the hearts and memories of thousands of American women, as one of our greatest and best." Catt concluded with a hope that Virginians would "honor her memory by faithfully marching forward in the direction she so fearlessly led!" On October 20, 1936, Nancy Astor, Viscountess Astor, presented to the state on behalf of the Lila Meade Valentine Memorial Association a marble bas-relief of Valentine by artist Harriet Frishmuth for installation in the chamber of the House of Delegates. It was the first and remains the only memorial to a woman inside the Virginia Capitol.[3]

Sophie Meredith's 1928 obituaries, though brief, focused on her suffragist career. She and several other members of the National Woman's Party in Virginia supported Alice Paul's campaign early in the decade for an amendment to the Constitution of the United States to guarantee full equal rights for women throughout the country. Meredith worked closely with Paul to have the Equal Rights Amendment passed because she believed that securing the vote for women was merely a first step and

The memorial to Lila Meade Valentine sculpted by Harriet Frishmuth is the only memorial to a woman inside the Virginia Capitol. *Library of Virginia.*

not enough to ensure gender equality. Meredith served on the advisory board of the National Woman's Party and as president of the Virginia branch until her death in August 1928. Her descendants carefully preserved Meredith's personal papers, which included the original state records of the Congressional Union/ National Woman's Party. The Library of Virginia digitized the party records.[4]

Meredith's best-known ally, Pauline Adams, remained an active member of the National Woman's Party for years and studied law and passed the bar examination in 1921. She ran unsuccessfully for the Norfolk City Council in 1923 and that same year campaigned for Fain during her first run for the House of Delegates. Adams's suffrage career and time in jail became a permanent part of the state's and city's histories long before she died in 1957. A small collection of her personal papers is in the Library of Virginia.[5]

Richmond banker Maggie Lena Walker did not run for public office again after the 1921 campaign, but she remained as active in African American women's organizations, both state and national, as she had been for decades until a stroke confined her to a wheelchair in 1928. She was one of the most famous businesswomen in the country. At the time of her death in 1934, the Independent Order of St. Luke had more than 100,000 members nationwide, a headquarters building valued at more than $100,000, about 200 employees, and 15,000 children enrolled in its thrift clubs. Virginia Union University granted her an honorary master of science degree, and the City of Richmond declared October 1934 as Maggie L. Walker Month. The superintendent of schools gave African American students in the city half a day off on the day of her funeral.[6]

Emma Kelley of Norfolk held office in the Daughters of the Improved Benevolent and Protective Order of Elks of the World until her death in 1932. The Daughters awarded her the honorary title Supreme Mother in 1923. She prospered and traveled throughout the country and in the West

Indies founding temples and overseeing their work. In 1926, Kelley published *Kelley's History of the Daughters of I.B.P.O.E.W.* Her daughter published revised editions in 1943 and 1961 and succeeded her as Grand Daughter Secretary of the order. She later established the Emma V. Kelley Memorial Scholarship at Queen Street Baptist Church.[7]

The Virginia Department of Education took over basic responsibilities for Janie Porter Barrett's Virginia Industrial School for Colored Girls in 1920, but she continued to manage it until she retired in 1940. "We explain the purpose and functioning of the ballot," she wrote in the school's 1938 annual report, "and teach that voting is a duty as well as a right. We use every opportunity and every device at our command to inspire patriotism, knowing that, with all its faults, our country is a much better place to live in than others of which we read, and believing that unfavorable conditions may be improved in proportion as clear thinking citizens participate actively in its affairs." During the 1920s, Barrett was an active member of the Virginia Commission on Interracial Cooperation and also of the Richmond Urban League. She served for four years as chair of the executive board of the National Association of Colored Women. Barrett retired in 1940, and two years later the General Assembly renamed her school the Janie Porter Barrett School for Girls. Barrett lived until 1948.[8]

Josephine Norcom, formerly of Portsmouth, joined a Newport News branch of the Woman's Republican League and attended its conference in Washington, D.C., in the autumn of 1920, even before she cast her first vote. She taught school and served on the board of managers of the Virginia Industrial School for Colored Girls. Norcom left Virginia about 1922 to work as the executive secretary of the YWCA in Cincinnati, Ohio. She held the same post in Detroit, Michigan, until her death in 1927. The Detroit YWCA established Camp Norcom for African American girls in 1928, in Dexter, Michigan.[9]

In addition to being the founding president of the Negro Women Voters' League of Virginia, Ora Brown Stokes was active in Republican Party politics in Virginia and spoke out forcefully against the party's neglect of African Americans. She directed the African American women's committee in the presidential campaign of 1924 in Virginia. Stokes served as president of the Southeastern Section of the National Association of Colored Women in the 1920s. She also served on the board of visitors of Hartshorn College, an African American women's school in Richmond that later became a part of Virginia Union University. Stokes earned a law degree from the short-lived law school at the university. Late in the 1930s, she was a special advisor on woman's work for the National Youth Administration in Washington, D.C., and later worked as a field director for the Woman's Christian Temperance Union and was the only African American member of its national staff. While working in Texas, she married a second time and later moved to St. Louis, Missouri, where she died in 1948.[10]

The two young paid organizers for the National American Woman Suffrage Association, Mary Elizabeth Pidgeon and Eudora Ramsay, had long and important professional careers ahead of them when the suffrage campaign came to its end in 1920. Pidgeon continued her work with the School of Citizenship at the University of Virginia until 1926. She completed a master's degree in political science at the University of Virginia in 1924 and also studied at the Fédération Universitaire Internationale, in Geneva, Switzerland, and at the University of Chicago. In 1928, Pidgeon moved to Washington, D.C., as assistant editor of the Women's Bureau of the Department of Labor. Promoted in 1930 to director of the bureau's Division of Research, she worked there until 1956. While Pidgeon was with the division, the bureau issued about two hundred official reports as separate issues of its influential *Bulletin of the Women's Bureau*. She was sole or principal author of about thirty reports on women in various workplace settings during the disruptive Great Depression, World War II and economic changes after the war. Pidgeon also was one of two dozen American women from various organizations who in 1936 wrote a women's charter as part of a campaign to secure for women full political and economic equality with men worldwide. She lived until November 1979.[11]

Eudora Ramsay married Fitzhugh Briggs Richardson, a Surry County attorney, in the autumn of 1917. They had met when she was speaking for woman suffrage earlier in the year. The marriage terminated her work on the road for woman suffrage. Eudora Ramsay Richardson thereafter devoted her career to ensuring that women embraced civic life. She was active in the Democratic Party and, as with every other cause, was diligent and unwavering. Richardson was well known as a writer. Her byline appeared in journals and newspaper columns across the country. In 1936, Richardson published *The Influence of Men—Incurable*, a response to John Erskine's book published earlier in the year, *The Influence of Women and Its Cure*. Richardson's book was a blend of historical research and political theory infused with social satire that articulated her complete and unwavering belief in women's equality with men. The book brought Richardson national acclaim and solidified her legacy as an influential feminist author. In 1937, she became state supervisor of the Virginia

Writers' Program. Part of the New Deal's Work Projects Administration, the program hired out-of-work teachers, journalists and writers to produce works that documented and shared Virginia history and culture. The Virginia Writers' Program was one of the best and most productive in the country. She retired in 1950 and died in 1973.[12]

Elizabeth Otey, after her first venture into elective politics, briefly returned to Bryn Mawr in 1923 as a tutor in economics. In 1924, the Christian Social Justice Fund published her short study *The Cotton Mill Workers on Jones Falls, Baltimore*. Otey traveled to Paris in 1926 with a small delegation from the National Woman's Party but failed to gain formal admittance to the International Woman Suffrage Alliance Congress. The national League of Women Voters (of which her mother was then state president) opposed admitting the National Woman's Party delegates in part because of the party's insistence on a declaration of full equality for men and women in public and economic life. Following the death of her husband in 1933, she returned to Washington, D.C., and worked for the Social Security Administration and later for the Foreign Economic Administration of the Department of State until she retired in 1948. Otey eventually returned to Virginia and died in Lynchburg in February 1974.[13]

Otey's mother, Elizabeth Lewis, lived until the last week of January 1946 and was the grandame of Lynchburg. In November 1920, at the formal founding meeting of the Virginia League of Women Voters, she was elected to the board of directors even though she was not present. She presided over the 1923 state convention and was elected president for the 1926–27 term. Lewis also served as the first president of the Lynchburg League of Women Voters from 1920 into the mid-1930s, when she was in her eighties. In 1931, the Virginia league added Lewis's name to the honor roll of the national league in recognition of her many years of work on behalf of woman suffrage and the League of Women Voters. Lewis traveled to Richmond early in 1926 to present to the state museum a set of suffrage banners, including the Lynchburg league's banner. (The banners were apparently lost after the closing of the museum in the 1960s.) Lady Astor visited her in Lynchburg late in January 1946, but Lewis was too weak to attend a delayed public celebration of her ninety-fourth birthday with her niece. Lewis died shortly after Astor left town.[14]

Jessie Townsend presided at the founding meeting of the League of Women Voters in the Capitol in November 1920, served on the committee that drafted its constitution, and was elected first vice president. The 1926 state convention honored her with a silver loving cup. Townsend was also

In 1923, Adèle Clark (*second from left*) and other members of the League of Women Voters met with Senators Claude Swanson and Carter Glass. *VCU Libraries.*

active in other civic capacities. She served as chair of Norfolk's Committee on the Cause and Cure of War and helped plan study classes and meetings in the city with representatives from other women's organizations. Townsend also worked with the city's public library to add books on international affairs to its collection. She died in 1941.[15]

Adèle Clark lived until 1983. Of all the suffragists, she had the most conspicuous public career. Elected the first president of the Virginia League of Women Voters in 1920, she served until 1925 and again from 1929 to 1944, and during the intervening years she was vice president of the national league. Even as Clark remained active in the Richmond arts community and as an art teacher, she served on two gubernatorial committees on government simplification in the 1920s and was state director of the Federal Art Project, a New Deal agency, in the 1930s. As a lifelong advocate for women, she was a founder in 1923 of the Virginia Women's Council of Legislative Chairmen of State Organizations. Clark was much in the news during the campaign in the 1970s to ratify the Equal Rights Amendment to the Constitution of the United States. She had opposed the National Woman's Party's attempt to amend the constitution in the 1920s for fear that legislation adopted to benefit women might suffer, and she remained consistent and opposed the new amendment for the same reason in the 1970s. Clark's abundant personal papers include a large quantity of Equal Suffrage League correspondence and numerous photographs and are in the library of Virginia Commonwealth University in Richmond. The Virginia Women's Monument dedicated in October 2019 on the grounds of the state capitol featured a bronze statue of Clark carrying a woman suffrage banner.[16]

Clark's sister, Edith Clark Cowles, continued her public involvement in civic affairs involving women and children. Cowles was a founder of the Lewis Ginter Library at the Ginter Park Community House, in Richmond, which opened in February 1923. She served as librarian and executive secretary of the Community House for twenty-three years. Cowles also wrote the eight-page history of the campaign for woman suffrage in Virginia for the sixth and final volume of *History of Woman Suffrage* (1922). Her chapter included background on the two failed nineteenth-century attempts to create a woman suffrage movement in Virginia and useful details about the work of the Equal Suffrage League of Virginia. She completely ignored African Americans and the issue of race. Reflecting the hard feelings that arose between leaders of the league and the National Woman's Party, the account virtually ignored the Virginians who joined the party. The only reference to the existence of the National Woman's Party is a two-sentence criticism of the party's failed attempt to have the August 1919 special session of the General Assembly ratify the Nineteenth Amendment. "Spurred on, however, by efforts of the National Woman's Party to secure action at any cost," Cowles wrote, "the opponents succeeded in having a Rejection Resolution railroaded through the House without debate ten minutes before adjournment in the second week of the session. The Senate refused to sanction such tactics and by 19 to 15 voted to postpone action until the next session." Cowles's chapter concluded with a short paragraph about passage of the proposed amendment to the state constitution, but later historians neglected that important episode or missed its significance.[17]

Ida Mae Thompson easily made the transition from secretary and office manager of the Equal Suffrage League in the autumn of 1920 to the same job with the Virginia League of Women Voters. In 1936 and 1937, she sought to gather into one place all the surviving records of the Equal Suffrage League. It is possible that she had most of the office files in her possession or that they were in the office of the League of Women Voters. Thompson was then working with University of Virginia archivist Lester

J. Cappon, who directed the Historical Records Survey in the state for the federal government's Work Projects Administration. Thompson started with the typed office memoranda that included names of local league officers and wrote to people throughout the state to ask them to help her gather and preserve records of their local leagues. That was probably when she obtained the many letters Valentine wrote to Lewis during the 1910s. Thompson also acquired from Townsend a large number of letters and documents, including Valentine's letters to Townsend, as well as minute books and other records of the Equal Suffrage League of Norfolk, a short history of the Norfolk league that Townsend wrote and a small quantity of Townsend's own personal papers. Townsend's disapproval of the radicalism of Pauline Adams led to a permanent estrangement between them, which must have created problems when they lived next door to each other for a time about 1930. "I have not asked Mrs Adams" for records, Townsend informed Thompson late in 1936, "thinking she would be eager to incorporate militant ideas and acts. They tell me she was the real originator of the work here but that is about all we need to say."[18]

The responses Thompson received from her letters of inquiry also brought some valuable and vivid recollections of the campaign for votes for women, which she added to the collection even if her correspondents had no original documents to submit. How or why Thompson's friend Adèle Clark kept and did not provide her the abundant league correspondence in her possession is not known. In 1942, Thompson deposited all the records she had preserved and collected in the Virginia State Library, which in 1994 the General Assembly renamed the Library of Virginia. It is one of the largest collections of woman suffrage records in any state.

VIRGINIA RATIFIES THE NINETEENTH AMENDMENT IN 1952

Woman suffrage got into the constitution of Virginia incrementally. Ratification of the Nineteenth Amendment in 1920 made irrelevant the amendment to the state constitution the General Assembly proposed that year, and in 1922 the legislators neglected to approve it again and submit it to a ratification referendum. In 1927, voters ratified a different amendment that for the first time constitutionally recognized woman suffrage in the state, but it in fact benefitted only a small number of women. The Virginia Constitution of 1902 had exempted men who had served in the United States or Confederate States armies and navies during the Civil War from paying a poll tax as a prerequisite for registering to vote. In 1927, sixty-two years after the end of the war, voters ratified an amendment to Article II, Section 22, that extended that exemption to "the wife or widow of such person." A comprehensive constitutional revision that the General Assembly proposed and voters ratified in 1928 eliminated the word *male* from the description of persons who could qualify to vote and added to Article II, Section 18, a new sentence adapted from the Nineteenth Amendment: "The right of citizens to vote shall not be denied or abridged on account of sex." That brought the state constitution into conformity with the national constitution.[19]

Members of the General Assembly of Virginia finally ratified the Nineteenth Amendment in February 1952. An undocumented story that has occasionally circulated since that time related that the daughter of an unidentified member of the assembly told her father that she had learned in school that Virginia had not ratified the amendment and asked why. He decided to change that. At the 1952 session of the assembly, fifteen male members of the House of Delegates sponsored a resolution to ratify the amendment. It passed the House of Delegates by a vote of 88 to 1 (11 members absent or not voting) on February 14, 1952, and the Senate by a vote of 30 to 0 (10 members absent or not voting) on February 21. Among the members of the Senate who voted to ratify the Nineteenth Amendment in 1952 was Harry Flood Byrd Jr., namesake son of the state senator who had opposed woman suffrage before 1920 and voted against the Nineteenth Amendment in that year. If there is a kernel of truth in the old story, then it was a Virginia schoolgirl whose teacher told her about the refusal of the General Assembly to ratify the Nineteenth Amendment in 1919 and 1920 who was ultimately responsible for the assembly's ratification of it thirty-one and a half years after it had become part of the Constitution of the United States.[20]

Appendix

VIRGINIA SUFFRAGISTS
AND ANTI-SUFFRAGISTS

Online Biographies in the *Dictionary of Virginia Biography*
(www.lva.virginia.gov/public/dvb)

The *Dictionary of Virginia Biography* is an ongoing biographical reference work published by the Library of Virginia covering all centuries, regions and categories of Virginia's history and culture and highlighting many Virginians whose lives have rarely been studied.

SUFFRAGE ACTIVISTS

Pauline Forstall Colclough Adams (1874–1957), Norfolk
Lillie Mary Barbour (1885–1985), Roanoke
Edmonia Carter Powers Barksdale (1847–1918), Richmond
Janie Porter Barrett (1865–1948), Hampton and Hanover County
Katherine Harwood Waller Barrett (d. 1925), Alexandria
Anna Whitehead Bodeker (1826–1904), Richmond
Kate Lee Langley Bosher (1865–1932), Richmond
Jane Rhea Bailey Byars (1872–1948), Arlington County
Adèle Clark (1882–1983), Richmond
Mary Ellen Pollard Clarke (1862–1939), Richmond
Edith Clark Cowles (1874–1954), Richmond

Janet Stuart Oldershaw Durham (1879–1969), Richmond

Janetta R. FitzHugh (1866–1950), Fredericksburg

Ellen Anderson Gholson Glasgow (1873–1945), Richmond

Nora Houston (1883–1942), Richmond

Elizabeth Aymar Cooke Hull (1893–1979), Norfolk

Maud Powell Jamison (1890–1974), Norfolk

Julia Somerville Jennings (1860–1933), Richmond

Mary Eugenia Benson Jobson (1872–1962), Richmond

Mary Johnston (1870–1936), Richmond and Bath County

Emma Virginia Lee Kelley (1867–1932), Norfolk

Ellen Gertrude Tompkins Kidd (d. 1932), Richmond

Fannie Stratton Bayly King (1864–1951), Staunton

Orra Henderson Moore Gray Langhorne (1841–1904), Lynchburg

Marie Leahey (1869–1951), Richmond

Elizabeth Dabney Langhorne Lewis (1851–1946), Lynchburg

Mary Morris Hall Lockwood (1871–1936), Arlington County

Lucy Randolph Mason (1882–1959), Richmond

Sarah Mason Sandridge Matthews (1881–1963), Norfolk and Charlottesville

Marianne Everard Meade (1876–1970), Richmond

Sophie Gooding Rose Meredith (1851–1928), Richmond

Kate Noble Pleasants Minor (1857–1925), Richmond

Faith Walcott Morgan (1869–1964), Hampton

Mary-Cooke Branch Munford (1866–1938), Richmond

Josephine B. Mathews Norcom (1873–1927), Portsmouth

Elizabeth Dabney Langhorne Lewis Otey (1880–1974), Lynchburg

Millie Lawson Bethell Paxton (1875–1939), Roanoke

Mary Elizabeth Pidgeon (1890–1979), Clarke County

Betty Ellison Withers Putney (1858–1918), Wytheville

Agnes Dillon Randolph (1875–1930), Richmond

Eudora Woolfolk Ramsay Richardson (1891–1973), Richmond

Sally Berkeley Nelson Robins (1855–1925), Richmond

Ellen Llewellyn Robinson (1872–1923), Newport News

Ora E. Brown Stokes (1882–1957), Richmond

Alice B. Overbey Taylor (1879–1919), Richmond

Lucinda Lee Terry (1873–1957), Roanoke

Ida Mae Thompson (1866–1947), Richmond

Jessie Fremont Easton Townsend (1861–1941), Norfolk

Lila Hardaway Meade Valentine (1865–1921), Richmond

Maggie Lena Mitchell Walker (1864–1934), Richmond

Roberta Wellford (1873–1956), Richmond and Charlottesville
Annie S. Barna Whitner (1870–1960), Roanoke
Louise Price Collier Willcox (1865–1929), Norfolk
Sarah Blair Harvie Wormeley (1869–1964), Richmond
Eugénie Macon Yancey (1866–1947), Bedford

SUFFRAGE OPPONENTS

Jane Meade Rutherfoord (1840–1918), Richmond
Molly Elliot Seawell (1853–1916), Gloucester County
Mary Mason Anderson Williams (1871–1945), Richmond

FIRST WOMEN IN THE GENERAL ASSEMBLY

Sallie Cook Booker (1857–1944), Henry County
Nancy Melvina "Vinnie" Caldwell (1868–1956), Carroll County
Sarah Lee Odend'hal Fain (1888–1962), Norfolk
Helen Moore Timmons Henderson (1877–1925), Buchanan County
Helen Ruth Henderson (1898–1982), Buchanan County
Emma Lee Smith White (1881–1983), Mathews County

NOTES

Abbreviations and Short Titles

Clark Papers
Adèle Goodman Clark papers, Collection M 9, Special Collections and Archives, James Branch Cabell Library, Virginia Commonwealth University, Richmond, Va.

CU Minute Book
Congressional Union, Virginia Branch, Minute Book (1915–1920), Accession 52758, Library of Virginia, Richmond, Va.

ESL
Equal Suffrage League of Virginia Records, Accession 22002, Library of Virginia, Richmond, Va.

NWP Papers
National Woman's Party Papers, Library of Congress, Washington, D.C.

Online *DVB*
Dictionary of Virginia Biography (Library of Virginia, 1998–), accessible at the Library of Virginia website (www.lva.virginia.gov/public/dvb)

Chapter 1. Let Our Vote Be Cast: An Introduction

1. Conversation quoted in *Virginian-Pilot and Norfolk Landmark*, Nov. 3, 1920.
2. *Richmond Times-Dispatch*, Jan. 1, 1915, quotation.
3. *Philadelphia Tribune*, Aug. 13, 1921, quotation.
4. *St. Luke Herald*, Apr. 4, 1914, quotation.

Chapter 2. No Woman Sole or Covert: Virginia Women and the Vote before 1920

1. J.R. Pole, "Representation and Authority in Virginia from the Revolution to Reform," *Journal of Southern History* 24 (1958): 16–50; J.R. Pole, *Political Representation in England and the Origins of the American Revolution* (London, 1966); Jackson Turner Main, *The Upper House in Revolutionary America, 1763–1788* (Madison: University of Wisconsin Press, 1967); Gordon S. Wood, *The Creation of the American Republic, 1776–1787* (Chapel Hill: University of North Carolina Press, 1969), 162–196, 206–226, 237–255; John Phillip Reid, *The Concept of Representation in the Age of the American Revolution* (Chicago: University of Chicago Press, 1989); Brent Tarter, "When Kind and Thrifty Husbands Are Not Enough: Some Thoughts on the Legal Status of Women in Virginia," *Magazine of Virginia Genealogy* 33 (1995): 79–101; Holly Brewer, *By Birth or Consent: Children, Law, and the Anglo-American Revolution in Authority* (Chapel Hill: University of North Carolina Press, 2005).
2. Governor Sir George Yeardley's 1618 instructions are evidently lost, but company officials copied them for Sir Francis Wyatt's use later. Susan Myra Kingsbury, ed., *Records of the Virginia Company*, 4 vols. (Washington, D.C., 1906–1935) 3:483–484, first quotation on 483, and Wyatt's warrant dated Jan. 26, 1624, 4:449, second quotation.
3. William Waller Hening, ed., *The Statutes at Large of Virginia…*, 13 vols. (Richmond, New York, and Philadelphia, 1809–1823), 2:280, 3:172–175, quotation on 172.
4. Hening, *Statutes at Large*, 3:236–246, 4:475–478.
5. Hening, *Statutes at Large*, 9:115, 349–368, quotation on 351.
6. Richard Henry Lee to Hannah Lee Corbin, Mar. 17, 1778, in James Curtis Ballagh, ed., *The Letters of Richard Henry Lee*, 2 vols. (New York, 1911–1914), 1:392–394, quotation on 393; Louise Belote Dawe and Sandra Gioia Treadway, "Hannah Lee Corbin, The Forgotten Lee,"

Virginia Cavalcade 29 (1979): 70–77; Cynthia A. Kierner, "Hannah Lee Corbin," online *DVB*; Hening, *Statutes at Large*, 10:501–517.

7. Poll list, quotations, Staunton City, Election Returns, Overseer of the Poor Papers, Local Government Records Collection, Library of Virginia.

8. *Debates and Proceedings of the Constitutional Convention of the State of Virginia* (Richmond, 1868), 467, quotation; Elsa Barkley Brown, "To Catch the Vision of Freedom: Reconstructing Southern Black Women's Political History, 1865–1880," in *African American Women and the Vote, 1837–1965*, ed. Ann D. Gordon et al. (Amherst: University of Massachusetts Press, 1997), 79–83.

9. Laura E. Free, *Suffrage Reconstructed: Gender, Race, and Voting Rights in the Civil War Era* (Ithaca, NY: Cornell University Press, 2015).

10. Sandra Gioia Treadway, "A Most Brilliant Woman: Anna Whitehead Bodeker and the First Woman Suffrage Association in Virginia," *Virginia Cavalcade* 43 (1994): 166–77; Sandra Gioia Treadway, "Anna Whitehead Bodeker," online *DVB*.

11. Frances S. Pollard, "Orra Henderson Moore Gray Langhorne," online *DVB*; Charles E. Wynes, ed., *Southern Sketches from Virginia, 1881–1901, Orra Langhorne* (Charlottesville: University Press of Virginia, 1964), quotation on xxviii.

12. *Journal of the House of Delegates*, 1879–1880 sess., quotation on 337.

13. National American Woman Suffrage Association *Proceedings* (1898), 112, quotation.

14. *Acts of the General Assembly*, 1896 sess., 636–43, first quotation on 642, and 1904 sess., 947; *Salem Times-Register*, Apr. 13, 1911; *Staunton Daily Leader*, May 10, 1911, second quotation; Fredericksburg *Free Lance*, Apr. 13, May 11, 1911; *Staunton Dispatch-News*, May 14, 1911.

15. Washington *Sunday Star*, June 20, 1915; *Woman's Journal*, July 31, 1915; *Acts of the General Assembly*, 1916 sess., 28, quotation.

Chapter 3. Work Like Hell and Educate: The Equal Suffrage League of Virginia

1. *Year Book of the Equal Suffrage League of Virginia* (Richmond, 1910), 19, quotation; typed minutes, ESL; undated typed list of women at Nov. 20, 1909, meeting, Clark Papers.

2. Typed board of directors minutes, Jan. 6, 1910, quotation, ESL.

3. Barbara C. Batson, "Ellen Glasgow," and Brent Tarter, "Mary Johnston," both online *DVB*.

4. *Woman's Journal*, Dec. 17, 1910, quotation.

5. Brent Tarter, "Janetta R. FitzHugh," online *DVB*.

6. Stacy G. Moore, "Willie Brown Walker Caldwell," and Brent Tarter, "Lila Hardaway Meade Valentine," both online *DVB*.

7. Benjamin B. Valentine to Lila Meade Valentine, Aug. 8, 1913, quotation, Lila Meade Valentine Papers, Virginia Historical Society.

8. Lila Meade Valentine typescript speech, Sept. 7, 1916, quotations, ESL.

9. Frances S. Pollard, "Ellen Gertrude Tompkins Kidd," online *DVB*.

10. Jennifer Davis McDaid, "Adèle Clark," online *DVB*

11. Frances S. Pollard, "Nora Houston," online *DVB*.

12. Kelley M. Ewing, "Edith Clark Cowles," online *DVB*; *Richmond Times-Dispatch*, Sep. 23, 1917, quotation.

13. Grayson Katzenbach, "Fannie Stratton Bayly King," online *DVB*.

14. Leila Christenbury, "Agnes Dillon Randolph," online *DVB*.

15. Diane McVittie Reukauf, "Katherine Harwood Waller Barrett," online *DVB*.

16. Marianne E. Julienne, "Lillie Mary Barbour," online *DVB*; *Richmond Times-Dispatch*, Jan. 1, 1915, quotation.

17. Leila Christenbury, "Edmonia Carter Powers Barksdale," online *DVB*; *Richmond Times-Dispatch*, and Richmond *Evening Journal*, both Feb. 13, 1914, quotation.

18. Jennifer Ritterhouse, "Lucy Randolph Mason," online *DVB*; Lucy Randolph Mason to Lila Meade Valentine, Jan. 10, 1911 (photocopy), quotation, Betsy Brinson Papers, 1894–1999, Concerning the History of Women in Virginia and the South, Virginia Historical Society.

19. Nancy Alexander Simmons, "Betty Ellison Withers Putney," online *DVB*; Ellie Putney to unidentified recipient, Feb. 8, 1912, quotation, ESL.

20. Sallie J. Miles to Lila Meade Valentine, Apr. 13, 1919, quotation, ESL.

21. Brent Tarter, "Elizabeth Dabney Langhorne Lewis," online *DVB*; "A Confession of Faith," *Virginia Suffrage News* 1 (Nov. 1914), quotation.

22. Brent Tarter, "Louise Price Collier Willcox," online *DVB*; *Harper's Weekly* 57 (Aug. 9, 1913): 5, quotation.

23. Jennifer Davis McDaid, "Pauline Forstall Colclough Adams," online *DVB*.

24. Laura Davenport to Ida M. Thompson, Mar. 10, 1937, quotation, Equal Suffrage League of Tazewell Co. Records, ESL.

25. *The Remonstrance*, Apr. 1912, quotation.

26. Lida R. Crabell to Ida M. Thompson, Mar. 12, 1937, first quotation, Equal Suffrage League of Carroll Co. Records, and Ellie Putney to Alice Tyler, May 23, 1912, third quotation, both ESL; Fredericksburg *Free Lance*, Feb. 4, 1911, second quotation; M.S. Yost to Miss Ryan, Aug. 16, 1913, National American Woman Suffrage Association Papers, Library of Congress, container 30, fourth quotation.

27. Fannie B. King to Miss Thompson, n.d. [ca. 1936–37], first quotation, Equal Suffrage League of Staunton Records, ESL; *Richmond Times-Dispatch*, Dec. 10, 1915, second quotation.

28. John G. Deal, "Jane Meade Rutherfoord," online *DVB*; *Tenth Annual Report of the Woman's Club, March 1904* (Richmond, 1904), 6, quotation.

29. Kimberly R. Bowman, "Mary Mason Anderson Williams," online *DVB*; James Michael Lindgren, *Preserving the Old Dominion: Historic Preservation and Virginia Traditionalism* (Charlottesville: University of Virginia Press, 1993).

30. Brent Tarter, "Molly Elliot Seawell," online *DVB*; "On the Absence of the Creative Faculty in Women," *The Critic: A Weekly Review of Literature and the Arts* 16 (1891): 292–94, quotation on 292.

31. Adèle Clark, "The Suffragist Movement: A Reply to Miss Molly Elliot Seawell," *Richmond Times-Dispatch*, Mar. 11, 1912, reprinted as *Facts vs. Fallacies: Anti-Suffrage Allegations Refuted* (Richmond, 1912); Molly Elliot Seawell, "Two Suffrage Mistakes," *North American Review* 199 (1914): 366–82.

32. Sara Hunter Graham, "Woman Suffrage in Virginia: The Equal Suffrage League and Pressure-Group Politics, 1909–1920," *Virginia Magazine of History and Biography* 101 (1993): 227–49; Suzanne Lebsock, "Woman Suffrage and White Supremacy: A Virginia Case Study," in *Visible Women, New Essays on American Activism*, ed. Nancy A. Hewitt and Suzanne Lebsock (Urbana: University of Illinois Press, 1993); Marjorie Spruill Wheeler, *New Women of the New South: The Leaders of the Woman Suffrage Movement in the Southern States* (New York: OUP USA, 1993); Elna C. Green, *Southern Women and the Woman Suffrage Question* (Chapel Hill: University of North Carolina Press, 1997).

33. Brent Tarter, *The Grandees of Government: The Origins and Persistence of Undemocratic Politics in Virginia* (Charlottesville: University of Virginia Press, 2013), 265–273.

34. Lila Meade Valentine to Jessie Townsend, Apr. 10, 1915, and to Mary Elizabeth Pidgeon, Oct. 11, 1919, both ESL.

35. *The Crisis* 8 (July 1914): 145–46; Lebsock, "Woman Suffrage and White Supremacy," 69.

36. *St. Luke Herald*, June 6, 1914, quotation.
37. *Southern Workman* 41 (1912): 536, first quotation, 539, 542; *Minutes of the Eighth Biennial Convention of the National Association of Colored Women* (1912): 10, 58, second quotation.
38. *National Association Notes* 16 (June 1913): 4–8, quotations on 7.
39. Quoted in *The Crisis* 6 (May 1913): 21, first quotation, and 7 (April 1914): 278, second quotation.
40. *St. Luke Herald*, May 23, 1914, first quotation; *Newport News Star*, July 12, 1918, second quotation, Peabody Clippings, William R. and Norma B. Harvey Library, Hampton University.
41. Anne Firor Scott, "Janie Aurora Porter Barrett," online *DVB*.
42. Alice O. Taylor to Mrs. John H. Lewis, May 4, 1915, quotation, ESL; *Richmond Times-Dispatch*, May 2, 1915.
43. City of Norfolk Office Chief of Police permit, Feb. 10, 1913, quotation, Wyndham R. Mayo to Jessie E. Townsend, May 15, 1915, Equal Suffrage League of Norfolk annual report, Oct. 1916, Equal Suffrage League of Norfolk Records, all ESL.
44. *Woman's Journal*, Sept. 18, 1915, quotation.
45. Ms postscript to typescript annual report 1916–1917 signed M.J.P., first quotation, Equal Suffrage League of Albemarle Co. Records, unsigned undated pencil notations on verso of Ida M. Thompson to Fanny M. Walcott, Nov. 17, 1936, second quotation, Equal Suffrage League of Hampton Records, both ESL; *Richmond Times-Dispatch*, Feb. 5, 1943, third quotation.

Chapter 4. Everlastingly At It: Organizing Virginia Suffragists

1. *Journal of the House of Delegates*, 1912 sess., 364.
2. Alice M. Tyler, Headquarters Report, Mar. 2, 1912, quotation, ESL.
3. Alice M. Tyler circular letter, Mar. 1912, quotation, ESL.
4. Equal Suffrage League Bulletin, July 1916, quotation, ESL.
5. Lila Meade Valentine to Alice Tyler, Oct. 9, 1912, quotation, and Bristol Equal Suffrage League Records, both ESL.
6. Mrs. J.C. Morehead to Mrs. Valentine, Jan. 9, 1915, quotation, Equal Suffrage League of Pulaski Records, ESL.
7. Lila Meade Valentine to Elizabeth Lewis, June 23, 1915, quotation, ESL.
8. I[da]. M. T[hompson]. to Judge P. H. Dillard, June 22, 1916, quotation, ESL.
9. Kathryn Gehred, "Eugénie Macon Yancey," online *DVB*; undated Biographical Sketches, quotation, ESL.

10. Elizabeth Otey to Miss Thompson, July 6, 1916, quotations, ESL.

11. Brent Tarter, "Elizabeth Dabney Langhorne Lewis Otey," online *DVB*.

12. Frances S. Pollard, "Marianne Everard Meade," online *DVB*; Equal Suffrage League Headquarters Report, Jan. 4, 1917, quotation, ESL.

13. Undated list enclosed in Lila Meade Valentine to Mrs. John H. Lewis, July 2, 1915, first quotation, ESL; Lila Meade Valentine to Mrs. Fillmore Tyson, Apr. 3, 1916, second quotation, Clark Papers.

14. Brent Tarter, "Alice B. Overbey Taylor," online *DVB*; *Richmond Times-Dispatch*, July 24, 1913, quotations.

15. Jennifer R. Loux, "Mary Ellen Pollard Clarke," online *DVB*.

16. Lila Meade Valentine to Jessie Townsend, Jan. 11, 1915, first quotations, and Sept. 14, 1915, second quotation, both ESL.

17. Jennifer Davis McDaid, "Ida Mae Thompson," online *DVB*.

18. Margaret Rhett, "Faith Walcott Morgan," online *DVB*.

19. Brent Tarter, "Ellen Llewellyn Robinson," online *DVB*; Faith W. Morgan, annual report, Dec. 8, 1915, quotation, Equal Suffrage League of Newport News Records, ESL.

20. Andrea Ledesma, "Eudora Woolfolk Ramsay Richardson," online *DVB*; Lila Meade Valentine to Jessie Townsend, Nov. 9, 1915, quotations, ESL.

21. *Richmond Times-Dispatch*, Dec. 9, 1915, quotation.

22. Janetta R. FitzHugh to Ida M. Thompson, Jan. 16, 1937, quotation, Equal Suffrage League of Fredericksburg Records, ESL.

23. Lynchburg Equal Suffrage League annual report, Nov. 7, 1914, quotations, Equal Suffrage League of Lynchburg Records, ESL.

24. Jennifer Davis McDaid, "Jessie Fremont Easton Townsend," online *DVB*.

25. Equal Suffrage League of Norfolk annual report, n.d., [1912], quotation, Equal Suffrage League of Norfolk Records, ESL.

26. Equal Suffrage League of Norfolk annual report, Nov. 6, 1914, quotation, Equal Suffrage League of Norfolk Records, ESL.

27. Undated manuscript on Equal Suffrage League of Virginia letterhead, National American Woman Suffrage Association Papers, container 76, quotations, Library of Congress.

28. Equal Suffrage League of Virginia Bulletin, Aug. 1916, quotation, ESL.

29. Faith W. Morgan to Madame President, Dec. 8, 1915, quotation, Equal Suffrage League of Newport News Records, ESL.

30. Equal Franchise League of Roanoke annual report docketed 1915 and identified as by "Mrs. Burks," quotation, Equal Franchise League of Roanoke Records, ESL.

31. Brent Tarter, "Annie S. Barna Whitner," online *DVB*; *Virginia Suffrage News* (Nov. 1914), 10, quotation.

32. Barbara C. Batson, "Lucinda Lee Terry," online *DVB*; Equal Suffrage League of Roanoke Co. annual report, n.d., docketed 1916–1917, quotation, ESL.

33. Equal Suffrage League of Fredericksburg Records, first quotation; Equal Suffrage League of Campbell Co. Records, second quotation; Equal Suffrage League of Charlotte Co. Records, third quotation; Equal Suffrage League of Fluvanna Co. Records, fourth quotation; Equal Suffrage League of Brunswick Co. Records, fifth quotation, all ESL.

34. Equal Suffrage League of Martinsville Records, quotation, ESL.

35. Mrs. R.H. Woodward to Mrs. Blakey, May 6, 1916, first quotation, Clark Papers; Elizabeth Lewis to Lila Meade Valentine, Dec. 12, 1919, second quotation, and Annie Shackelford Smithey to Ida M. Thompson, Dec. 7, 1936, third quotation, Equal Suffrage League of Hanover Co. Records, both ESL.

36. Lalla Smoot to Mrs. Blakey, May 5, [1916?], quotation, Clark Papers.

37. *Big Stone Gap Post*, Apr. 12, 1916, quotation.

38. Equal Suffrage League of Virginia Bulletin, July 1916, quotation, ESL.

39. Equal Suffrage League of Williamsburg annual report docketed 1916–1917, quotation, Equal Suffrage League of Williamsburg Records, ESL.

40. Membership numbers in *Handbook of the National American Woman Suffrage Association* (1914), 181 (1916), 125, (1916), 202, (1917), 231; Lila Meade Valentine to Thadeus [*sic*] Caraway, Mar. 20, 1916, (quotation), ESL; *Journal of the House of Delegates*, 1912 sess., 364, 1914 sess., 872, 1916 sess., 601.

Chapter 5. Constant Agitation:
The Congressional Union/National Woman's Party

1. Liette Gidlow, "The Sequel: The Fifteenth Amendment, the Nineteenth Amendment, and Southern Black Women's Struggle to Vote," *Journal of the Gilded Age and Progressive Era* 17 (2018): 433–49.

2. Katherine H. Adams and Michael L. Keene, *Alice Paul and American Suffrage Campaign* (Urbana: University of Illinois Press, 2008), 9–15.

3. *Virginia Federation of Labor Journal* 2 (Mar. 1913), 12–13, first quotation; Morgan, undated memorandum, second quotation, ESL.

4. *The Crisis* 6 (1913): 296; Paula Giddings, *In Search of Sisterhood: Delta Sigma Theta and the Challenge of the Black Sorority Movement* (New York: William Morrow and Company, 1988), 55–60.

5. Marianne E. Julienne, "Mary Morris Hall Lockwood," online *DVB*; *Washington Herald*, Sept. 10, first and third quotations, 20, 1913; Washington *Evening Star*, Oct. 1, 1913, second quotation; Mary Lockwood to Alice M. Tyler, June 10, 1912, fourth quotation, ESL.

6. Mary Morris Lockwood to Mrs. Charles Boughton Wood, July 19, 1913, quotation, NWP Papers, 1913–1972, Library of Congress.

7. Alice Paul to Lila Meade Valentine, June 21, July 8, 12, 1913, second quotation, and Valentine to Paul, n.d. [ca. July 10, 1913], first quotation, both NWP Papers, 1913–1920.

8. Jennifer Davis McDaid, "Pauline Forstall Colclough Adams," online *DVB*.

9. Sophie Meredith Sides Cowan, "Sophie Gooding Rose Meredith," online *DVB*.

10. *Suffragist*, July 11, 1914; *Virginian-Pilot and Norfolk Landmark*, July 3, 1914, quotation.

11. *Richmond Times-Dispatch*, June 20, 1915, first quotation; *Suffragist*, June 12, 1915, second quotation.

12. *Suffragist*, June 26, 1915, quotation.

13. *Suffragist*, July 31, 1915, quotation.

14. *Suffragist*, Sept. 4, 1915, quotations.

15. *Suffragist*, Dec. 11, 1915, quotation.

16. Frances S. Pollard, "Julia Somerville Jennings," online *DVB*; Dear Suffragist, Mar. 24, 1916, quotation, ESL.

17. Meredith address June 28, 1916, quotations, tipped into CU Minute Book; membership reports in NWP Papers, 1913–1920.

18. *Woman's Journal*, Apr. 8, 1916.

19. Marianne E. Julienne, "Josephine Mathews Norcom," online *DVB*; *National Association Notes* 19 (Oct. 1916): 11, quotation.

20. *Fifteenth Annual Report of the Hampton Negro Conference* (Hampton, 1911), quotations on 50, 51–52, 54.

21. *National Association Notes* 19 (Jan. 1917): 3, quotation; mock election in *Southern Workman*, 45 (1916): 702.

22. CU Minute Book, 60–61; *Richmond Times-Dispatch*, Oct. 8. 1916, quotation.

23. *Hand Book of the National American Woman Suffrage Association Forty-Eighth Convention* (1916), 26, 39, 42, first quotation, 59, 66, second quotation, 68, third quotation.

24. Equal Suffrage League *Yearbook* (1916), 10, first quotation, 19, second quotation.

25. *Suffragist*, Jan. 17, 1917, quotation.

26. *Suffragist*, Jan. 17, 1917, first and second quotations; CU Minute Book, 67, third quotation.

27. *Suffragist*, Jan. 31, 1917, quotation.

28. *Virginian-Pilot and Norfolk Landmark*, Jan. 12, 1917, quotation.

29. Arthur S. Link et al., eds., *The Papers of Woodrow Wilson*, 69 vols. (Princeton, NJ: Princeton University Press, 1966–1994) 41:330, quotation.

30. Equal Suffrage League 1917–1919 Executive Secretary Report, quotation, ESL.

31. *Woman Citizen*, Oct. 27, 1917, quotation.

32. Doris Stevens, *Jailed for Freedom* (New York: Boni and Liveright, 1920), quotations on 84.

33. Lila Meade Valentine press release, July 2, 1917, quotation, ESL.

34. John G. Deal, "Maud Powell Jamison," online *DVB*.

35. *Suffragist*, July 28, 1917, first quotation, Sept. 1, 1917, second quotation.

36. Richmond *Evening Journal*, Aug. 28, 1917, first quotation; Louis Brownlow, *Passion for Anonymity: The Autobiography of Louis Brownlow, Second Half* (Chicago: University of Chicago Press, 1958), 78, second and third quotations.

37. *Suffragist*, Sept. 1, 1917, first quotation, Nov. 3, 1917, second quotation; *Hunter v. District of Columbia* 47 App D.C. 406.

38. Pauline Adams to Edward Forstall Adams, Sept. 30, 1917, third and fourth quotations, and to Walter P. Adams, Oct. 23, 1917, first and second quotations, Pauline Forestall Colclough Adams Papers, Library of Virginia.

39. Richmond *Evening Journal*, Oct. 24, 1917, quotation.

40. *Suffragist*, Dec. 1, 1917, quotation.

41. Executive Secretary to Mrs. L.S. Foster, Aug. 22, 1919, first quotation, and Equal Suffrage League 1917–1919 Executive Secretary Report, second quotation, both ESL.

42. *Suffragist*, Jan. 12, 1918, quotation.

43. Lynchburg *News*, Mar. 18, 1920, first quotation; Lila Meade Valentine to Jessie Townsend, Jan. 30, 1918, second quotation, ESL.

44. CU Minute Book, folded page n.d. [ca. 1919], quotation, with erroneous July instead of August.

45. *Papers of Woodrow Wilson*, 51:158, quotations.

46. *Suffragist*, Oct. 12, first quotation, Nov. 23, second quotation, 1918.

47. *Papers of Woodrow Wilson*, 53:277, first quotation; Stevens, *Jailed for Freedom*, 305, second quotation.
48. *Suffragist*, Feb. 15, 1919, quotation.
49. Lila Meade Valentine to Mrs. Halsey W. Wilson, Feb. 17, 1919, quotation, Clark Papers.
50. Jessie Townsend to Claude A. Swanson, June 27, 1918, telegram, quotation, Clark Papers.
51. *Papers of Woodrow Wilson*, 59:296, first quotation; *Richmond Times-Dispatch*, June 15, 1919, second quotation; illegible June 5, 1919, Richmond *Evening Journal* editorial quoted in *Suffragist*, July 5, 1919, third quotation.
52. Richmond *Evening Journal*, June 5, 1919, quotations.

Chapter 6. A Determined and Aggressive Lobby: Success in 1920

1. *The V.N. & I.I. Gazette* 26 (Jan. 1920): 20–27, quotations on 21, 24–25, 26.
2. *Suffragist*, Aug. 16, 1919, quotation.
3. Adèle Clark to Carrie Chapman Catt, Aug. 20, 1919, completed by Edith Clark Cowles, first quotation, ESL; Executive Secretary to Mrs. L.S. Foster, Aug. 22, 1919, second quotation, Clark Papers.
4. Woodrow Wilson to Benjamin Franklin Buchanan and to Harry R. Houston, both Aug. 22, 1919, *Papers of Woodrow Wilson*, 62:462, first quotation; Richmond *Evening Journal*, Aug. 30, 1919, second quotation
5. *Journal of the House of Delegates*, extra sess., 1919, 158, first quotation; *Journal of the Senate*, extra sess., 1919, 161, second quotation.
6. Edith Clark Cowles, "Virginia," in vol. 6 of *The History of Woman Suffrage* (Washington, D.C.: National American Woman Suffrage Association, 1922): 668, quotation.
7. Ibid.; Ellen Robinson to Ida Mae Thompson, Nov. 14, 1919, quotation, ESL.
8. Brent Tarter, "Mary Elizabeth Pidgeon," online *DVB*.
9. Ida Mae Thompson to Lila Meade Valentine, July 7, 1919, quotation, Clark Papers.
10. *Handbook of the National American Woman Suffrage Association* (Mar. 1919), 304.
11. *Richmond Times-Dispatch*, Aug. 5, 1919, quotation.
12. Lila Meade Valentine to Carrie Chapman Catt, Jan. 2, 1920, quotation, ESL.
13. Equal Suffrage League of Lynchburg annual report, Nov. 7, 1914, quotation, Equal Suffrage League of Lynchburg Records, ESL.

14. *Washington Post*, Feb. 4, 1920, quotation.

15. Index Cards Referencing Members of the General Assembly, 1919–1920, ESL.

16. Mary Elizabeth Pidgeon memorandum, Jan. 1920, headed Winchester, Senator Byrd, first quotation, with H.F. Byrd to E. Virginia Smith, Dec. 4, 1919, copy, second quotation, ESL.

17. Lila Meade Valentine to Mary Elizabeth Pidgeon, Oct. 11, 1919, quotation, ESL.

18. *Richmond Times-Dispatch*, Jan. 22, 1920; Lebsock, "Woman Suffrage and White Supremacy," 75.

19. Richmond *Evening Journal*, Jan. 21, 1920, quotations.

20. *Journal of the Senate*, 1920 sess., 173–74; *Journal of the House of Delegates*, 1920 sess., 272–73; *Richmond Times-Dispatch*, Feb. 8, 1920, quotation.

21. *Journal of the Senate*, 1920 sess., 515; *Journal of the House of Delegates*, 1920 sess., 806; *Acts of Assembly*, 1920 sess., 588–91.

22. *Journal of the Senate*, 1920 sess., 331–35; *Journal of the House of Delegates*, 1920 sess., 789–93; *Acts of Assembly*, 1920 sess., 523–27, quotations on 523, 524.

23. Lorraine Gates Schuyler, *The Weight of Their Votes: Southern Women and Political Leverage in the 1920s* (Chapel Hill: University of North Carolina Press, 2006), 198–99; undated typed press release, Clark Papers.

24. *Norfolk Ledger-Dispatch*, Mar. 13, 1920, quotation.

25. E[dith] C[lark] C[owles], Report of Executive and Press Secretary, Nov. 5, 1920, quotation, ESL.

Chapter 7. A Day of Triumph and Dignity: Virginia Women Vote

1. *Annual Report of the Attorney General to the Governor of Virginia for the Year 1920* (Richmond, 1921), 53–57, 72–75, 94, 96.

2. *Suffragist* 8 (Nov. 1920): 286; Hdq. Secty. [Ida Mae Thompson] to Jennie Moore, Aug 24, 1920, first quotation, Clark Papers; *Washington Post*, Aug. 22, 1920, second quotation; Chesterfield Co. registrar quoted by Hermine Moore, quoted in Lucy R. Mason to Edith Cowles, Sept. 21, 1920, Clark Papers, third quotation; Elizabeth W. Lewis to Headquarters, Sept. 9, 1920, Clark Papers, fourth quotation; Anne Harris to unidentified, Sept. 13, 1920, Clark Papers, fifth quotation; Frances S. Pollard, "Mary Eugenia Benson Jobson," and "Sarah Blair Harvie Wormeley," both online *DVB*.

3. Fanny Walcott quoted in F.W. Morgan to Headquarters, Sept. 24, 1920, Clark Papers.

4. Nannie Kent Ellis to Ida M. Thompson, Dec. 3, 1936, quotation, Equal Suffrage League of Montgomery Co. Records, ESL.

5. *Annual Report of the Attorney General to the Governor of Virginia for the Year 1920* (Richmond, 1921), 98–99, quotations.

6. *Acts of Assembly*, 1902, 3–4 sess., 564, first quotation; Henry W. Anderson, "Poplar Government in Virginia," *University of Virginia Record, Extension Series* 11 (June 1927): 66–68, second quotation.

7. Alexander quoted in C.C. Bly to Lila Meade Valentine, Sept. 22, 1920; first quotations, Ida Mae Thompson to Mrs. Lee, July 28, 1921, second quotation, both Clark Papers.

8. Richmond *Evening Journal*, Sept. 1, 1920, quotation.

9. Lauranett Lee, "Maggie Lena Walker," online *DVB*; Maggie Lena Walker Diary, Maggie Lena Walker National Historic Site, Richmond.

10. Ray Bonis, "Ora Brown Stokes," online *DVB*.

11. Margaret Edds, "Millie Lawson Bethell Paxton," online *DVB*.

12. Berryville *Courier*, Sept. 23, 1920, first quotation, clipping, Tuskegee Institute News Clippings File; Fanny Morgan Walcott to Headquarters, Sept. 8, 1920, second quotation, Clark Papers; Richmond *News Leader*, Sept. 17, 1920, third quotation.

13. *Richmond Times-Dispatch*, Sept. 19, 1920, quotation.

14. A.W. Hunton to Miss Ovington, Oct. 25, 1920, enclosing investigative reports, quotation, Administrative File, Discrimination Subject File, Voting Hampton Va., 1920, National Association for the Advancement of Colored People Papers, Library of Congress.

15. [Mary White Ovington?] to Harriet Stanton Blatch, Dec. 3, 1920, quotation, National Woman's Party Subject File in National Association for the Advancement of Colored People Papers, Library of Congress.

16. Norfolk *Journal and Guide*, Nov. 6, 1920, quotation, Tuskegee Institute News Clippings File; Lorraine Gates Schuyler, *The Weight of Their Votes: Southern Women and Political Leverage in the 1920s* (Chapel Hill: University of North Carolina Press, 2006), 53.

17. Margaret Edds, "Emma Virginia Lee Kelley," online *DVB*; A.B. Caldwell, ed., *History of the American Negro, Virginia Edition* (Atlanta, GA: A.B. Caldwell Publishing, 1921), 501, quotation.

18. *Richmond Planet*, Sept. 25, 1920, quotation.

19. Maggie L. Walker to Mrs. A.W. Hunton, Feb. 17, 1921, quotation, Women's Suffrage Subject File, National Association for the Advancement of Colored People Papers, Library of Congress.

20. Edgar Eugene Robinson, *The Presidential Vote, 1896–1932* (Stanford, CA: Stanford University Press, 1934), 354.

21. *Richmond Times-Dispatch*, Nov. 3, 1920, quotation.

22. *Norfolk Ledger-Dispatch*, Nov. 2, 1920, quotation.

23. *Virginian-Pilot and Norfolk Landmark*, Nov. 3, 1920, quotations.

24. *Roanoke Times*, Nov. 3, 1920, first quotation; Roanoke *World News* Nov. 4, 1920, second quotation; *Richmond Planet*, Nov. 13, 1920, third quotation.

25. *Richmond Times-Dispatch*, Nov. 3, 1920, quotations; Frances S. Pollard, "Marie Leahey," online *DVB*.

26. *Richmond Times-Dispatch*, Nov. 3, 1920, quotations.

27. Roanoke *World News*, Nov. 5, 1920, first quotation; Lynchburg *News*, Nov. 3, 1920, second quotation.

28. *Shenandoah Herald*, Nov. 5, 1920, first quotation; Fredericksburg *Daily Star*, Nov. 3, 1920, second quotation, and same story in Fredericksburg *Free Lance*, Nov. 4, 1920; Laura Davenport to Ida M. Thompson, Mar. 10, 1937, third quotation, Equal Suffrage League of Tazewell Co. Records, ESL; Newport News *Daily Press*, Nov. 3, 1920, fourth quotation.

29. W.J. Nelms to His Excellency Governor Westmoreland Davis, Apr. 23, 1921, quotation, Executive Papers of Governor Westmoreland Davis, Record Group 3, Library of Virginia.

30. Jessie Townsend to Cowles, "Norfolk 4-30 P.M. Tuesday" [Nov. 2, 1920], quotation, Clark Papers.

31. Richmond *Evening Dispatch*, Nov. 3, 1920, quotation.

32. *Richmond Times-Dispatch*, Nov. 3, 1920, quotation.

33. *Contested Election Case of Paul v. Harrison*, 67th Cong., 2d sess., House Report 1101; *Congressional Record*, 67th Cong., 4th sess., 545–547; these sources do not single out any particular issues relating to women; Gertrude W. Barton to Miss Thompson, Feb. 27, 1937, quotation, Equal Suffrage League of Winchester Records, ESL.

Chapter 8. The Rest of Their Lives: Virginia Women and the Vote after 1920

1. Election returns in *Annual Report of the Secretary of the Commonwealth…for the Year Ending September 30, 1921* (Richmond, 1922), 423–24.

2. Sandra G. Treadway and Marianne E. Julienne, "Sarah Lee Odend'hal Fain"; Brent Tarter, "Helen Moore Timmons Henderson"; John G. Deal, "Helen Ruth Henderson"; Brent Tarter, "Sallie Cook Booker"; Sandra

G. Treadway, "Nancy Melvina 'Vinnie' Caldwell"; and Kelly Kubiak, "Emma Lee Smith White," all online *DVB*.

3. Brent Tarter, "Lila Hardaway Meade Valentine," online *DVB*; typescript transcription of Carrie Chapman Catt to Adèle Clark, July 21, 1921 (quotation), Lila Meade Valentine Papers, Virginia Historical Society; *Ceremonies Unveiling the Portrait Tablet of Lila Meade Valentine: Hall of the House of Delegates, State Capitol, Richmond, Virginia. Tuesday, October 20, 1936, at 3:30 P.M.* (Richmond, 1926).

4. Sophie Meredith Sides Cowan, "Sophie Gooding Rose Meredith," online *DVB*.

5. Jennifer Davis McDaid, "Pauline Forstall Colclough Adams," online *DVB*.

6. Lauranett Lee, "Maggie Lena Walker," online *DVB*.

7. Margaret Edds, "Emma Virginia Lee Kelley," online *DVB*.

8. Anne Firor Scott, "Janie Aurora Porter Barrett," online *DVB*; *Twenty-Third Annual Report of the Virginia Industrial School for Colored Girls* (Richmond 1938), 9, quotation.

9. Marianne E. Julienne, "Josephine Mathews Norcom," online *DVB*.

10. Ray Bonis, "Ora Brown Stokes," online *DVB*.

11. Brent Tarter, "Mary Elizabeth Pidgeon," online *DVB*.

12. Andrea Ledesma, "Eudora Woolfolk Ramsay Richardson," online *DVB*.

13. Brent Tarter, "Elizabeth Dabney Langhorne Lewis Otey," online *DVB*.

14. Brent Tarter, "Elizabeth Dabney Langhorne Lewis," online *DVB*.

15. Jennifer Davis McDaid, "Jessie Freemont Easton Townsend," online *DVB*.

16. Jennifer Davis McDaid, "Adèle Clark," online *DVB*.

17. Kelley M. Ewing, "Edith Clark Cowles," online *DVB*; Cowles, "Virginia," in volume 6 of *History of Woman Suffrage*, 665–72, quotation on 670.

18. Jennifer Davis McDaid, "Ida Mae Thompson," online *DVB*; Jessie Townsend to Ida M. Thompson, Nov. 3, 1936, quotation, Equal Suffrage League of Norfolk Records, ESL.

19. Authenticated enrolled amendment, 1927 sess., chap. 5, and revised constitution, 1928 sess., chap. 46, both in Enrolled Bills, Records of the General Assembly, Record Group 78, Library of Virginia.

20. *Journal of the House of Delegates*, 1952 sess., 248, 363; *Journal of the Senate*, 1952 sess., 552.

SELECT BIBLIOGRAPHY

Primary

Adèle Clark oral history interview with Charlotte Shelton, August 15, 1973, RG 26/29, Albert and Shirley Small Special Collections Library, University of Virginia.

Adèle Goodman Clark Papers, James Branch Cabell Library, Virginia Commonwealth University.

Congressional Union and Woman's Party of Virginia Records, Library of Virginia, digitized and available free online as one of the Digital Collections on the Library of Virginia's Virginia Memory website, virginiamemory.com.

Elizabeth Lewis Otey oral history interview with Charlotte Shelton, August 7, 1973, RG 26/28, Albert and Shirley Small Special Collections Library, University of Virginia.

Equal Suffrage League of Virginia Records, Acc. 22002, Library of Virginia, digitized and available free online as one of the Digital Collections on the Library of Virginia's Virginia Memory website, virginiamemory.com.

Lila Meade Valentine Papers, Virginia Historical Society.

National American Woman Suffrage Association Records, 1839–1961, Library of Congress.

National Association for the Advancement of Colored People Papers, Series 4, Voting Rights Campaign, 1916–1950, Library of Congress.

National Woman's Party Papers, 1913–1974, Library of Congress.

Sophie Gooding Rose Meredith Papers, in possession of Sophie Meredith Sides Cowan, of Blue Hill, Maine, and Tucson, Arizona.

The Suffragist.

The Woman's Journal (until 1917), *The Woman Citizen* (beginning in June 1917).

Secondary

Brooks, Clayton McClure. "Escaping the Veritable Battle Cloud: Mary Johnston and the Reconstruction of History." *Virginia Magazine of History and Biography* 122 (2014): 336–67.

————. *The Uplift Generation: Cooperation across the Color Line in Early Twentieth-Century Virginia.* Charlottesville: University of Virginia Press, 2017.

Brown, Elsa Barkley. "To Catch the Vision of Freedom: Reconstructing Southern Black Women's Political History, 1865–1880." In *African American Women and the Vote, 1837–1965*, edited by Ann D. Gordon et al. Amherst: University of Massachusetts Press, 1997.

Cowles, Edith Clark. "Virginia." In volume 6 of *The History of Woman Suffrage*, edited by Ida Husted Harper. Washington, D.C.: National American Woman Suffrage Association, 1922.

Free, Laura E. *Suffrage Reconstructed: Gender, Race, and Voting Rights in the Civil War Era.* Ithaca, NY: Cornell University Press, 2015.

Gidlow, Liette. "The Sequel: The Fifteenth Amendment, the Nineteenth Amendment, and Southern Black Women's Struggle to Vote." *Journal of the Gilded Age and Progressive Era* 17 (2018): 433–49.

Graham, Sara Hunter. "Woman Suffrage in Virginia: The Equal Suffrage League and Pressure-Group Politics, 1909–1920." *Virginia Magazine of History and Biography* 101 (1993): 227–50.

Green, Elna C. *Southern Strategies: Southern Women and the Woman Suffrage Question.* Chapel Hill: University of North Carolina Press, 1997.

Kierner, Cynthia A., Jennifer R. Loux and Megan Taylor Shockley. *Changing History: Virginia Women through Four Centuries.* Richmond: Library of Virginia, 2013.

Lebsock, Suzanne. "Woman Suffrage and White Supremacy: A Virginia Case Study." In *Visible Women, New Essays on American Activism*, edited by Nancy A. Hewitt and Suzanne Lebsock. Urbana: University of Illinois Press, 1993.

McDaid, Jennifer Davis. "All Kinds of Revolutionaries: Pauline Adams, Jessie Townsend, and the Norfolk Equal Suffrage League." *Virginia Cavalcade* 49 (2000): 84–95.

Schuyler, Lorraine Gates. *The Weight of Their Votes: Southern Women and Political Leverage in the 1920s*. Chapel Hill: University of North Carolina Press, 2006.

Stevens, Doris. *Jailed for Freedom*. New York: Boni and Liveright, 1920.

Taylor, Lloyd C., Jr. "Lila Meade Valentine: The FFV as Reformer." *Virginia Magazine of History and Biography* 70 (1962): 471–87.

Treadway, Sandra G. "A Most Brilliant Woman: Anna Whitehead Bodeker and the First Woman Suffrage Association in Virginia," *Virginia Cavalcade* 43 (1994): 166–77.

Van Zelm, Antoinette G. "Orra Gray Langhorne, A Voice for Reform in Postbellum Virginia." In volume 2 of *Virginia Women, Their Lives and Times*, edited by Cynthia A. Kierner and Sandra Gioia Treadway. Athens: University of Georgia Press, 2015–2016.

We Demand: Women's Suffrage in Virginia. Website of the 2020 Library of Virginia exhibition on the Library of Virginia's Virginia Memory website, virginiamemory.com.

Wheeler, Marjorie Spruill. "Mary Johnston, Suffragist." *Virginia Magazine of History and Biography* 100 (1992): 99–118.

———. *New Women of the New South: The Leaders of the Woman Suffrage Movement in the Southern States*. New York: Oxford University Press, 1993.

Wynes, Charles E., ed. *Southern Sketches from Virginia, 1881–1901, Orra Langhorne*. Charlottesville: University Press of Virginia, 1964.

INDEX

ABOUT THE AUTHORS

Brent Tarter and Marianne E. Julienne are editors of the Library of Virginia's Dictionary of Virginia Biography project. Barbara C. Batson is exhibitions coordinator at the Library of Virginia.

Visit us at
www.historypress.com
....